So You Think
You Can Think

So You Think You Can Think

Tools for Having Intelligent Conversations and Getting Along

Christopher W. DiCarlo

ROWMAN & LITTLEFIELD
Lanham · Boulder · New York · London

160

Published by Rowman & Littlefield
An imprint of The Rowman & Littlefield Publishing Group, Inc.
4501 Forbes Boulevard, Suite 200, Lanham, Maryland 20706
www.rowman.com

6 Tinworth Street, London SE11 5AL, United Kingdom

British Library Cataloguing in Publication Information Available

Library of Congress Cataloging-in-Publication Data

Names: DiCarlo, Christopher, 1962– author.
Title: So you think you can think : tools for having intelligent conversations and
getting along / Christopher W. DiCarlo.
Description: Lanham : Rowman & Littlefield, 2020. | Includes bibliographical
references and index. | Summary: "This book offers the reader genuine hope
that civility has not been lost to blind, dogmatic beliefs in personal or political
ideology and that we can regain our sense of fairness and continue to have
discussions about important matters, disagree entirely, but still be able to get
along and appreciate discourse over hatred, dialogue over violence, and most
importantly, fairness and understanding in our disagreements on important
issues" — Provided by publisher.
Identifiers: LCCN 2019057259 (print) | LCCN 2019057260 (ebook) | ISBN
9781538138557 (cloth) | ISBN 9781538138564 (ebook)
Subjects: LCSH: Thought and thinking. | Courtesy. | Fairness. | Conduct of life.
Classification: LCC BF442 .D53 2020 (print) | LCC BF442 (ebook) | DDC
160—dc23
LC record available at https://lccn.loc.gov/2019057259
LC ebook record available at https://lccn.loc.gov/2019057260

This book is dedicated to all of my students—
past, present, and future.

Too often we give children answers to remember rather than problems to solve.

—Roger Levin

Contents

Acknowledgments

It does not require the wisdom of a sage to know that any accomplishment is the result of many people. And this book is of no exception. I am personally indebted to so many gifted and wonderful people who have shaped my understanding and encouraged my passion for education in the field of critical thinking. I would like to thank my past professors, especially people like Jakob Amstutz at the University of Guelph, whose discussion of Plato's *Apology* single-handedly convinced me to change my undergraduate major from English to philosophy. He, along with other professors at Guelph, such as Jay Newman, Doug Odegard, Helier Robinson, and Michael Ruse, made my learning experiences joyful, troubling, and without end. The same holds true for my doctoral years at the University of Waterloo. People like Jan Narveson, Bill Abbott, Rolf George, Don Roberts, Joe Novak, and my co-supervisors, Jim Van Evra and Michael Ruse, demonstrated considerable patience and insight during this time. In addition, I am grateful for the guidance and acceptance I received during my postdoctoral work in the Stone Age Laboratory at Harvard University. My host, Ofer Bar-Yosef, was always welcoming and gracious to me as well as my family. I thank David Pilbeam, Richard Wrangham, Brian Hare, and Steven Pinker for taking the time to have valuable discussions with me regarding cognitive evolution and human and animal reasoning. I must thank the thousands of students over the years whose inquisitiveness, sharpness, and intelligence have kept me accountable for my biases. I would also like to thank many friends and acquaintances whose good company, insights, and intelligence have nurtured my outlook on life and restored my faith in humanity. A special nod goes out to the boys in Mink's hut at the 14 1/2 M Street Debating Society; this good-natured forum has allowed for the development of ideas in ways no academic institution could have provided. I sure do miss those days. I would like to thank the illustrator of this book—Heather Thomson—who has done a magnificent job with the quality of the illustrations. A great deal of thanks also goes out to my literary agent, Mark Gottlieb at Trident Media Group, not only for his dedication to me as a writer but also to critical thinking writ large. In addition, a great deal of thanks goes to the folks at Rowman & Littlefield, especially copy editor, Bruce Owens; production editor, Melissa McNitt; and executive editor, Suzanne I. Staszak-Silva. And to my friend and journalist, Troy Bridgeman, I thank you for the time and devotion you have made and continue to make for responsible journalism and the teaching of critical thinking. I must also thank Kal Sayid and Lannie Le from *Pixel Dreams*. In their effort to raise intelligence and consciousness throughout the world, they have given me the freedom to creatively and critically think in an environment that is forward-thinking, cutting-edge, and realistic. The entire *Pixel Dreams* Team are an amazing bunch of people who genuinely care about important issues happening in real time. A great deal of thanks is owed to my family—both extended and nuclear. My dearly departed parents, Marjory and Ernest DiCarlo, have influenced me in so many ways. Their thoughtful guidance, patience, and respect have directed my understanding of the world in ways I am only now beginning to fathom. To my siblings, Brad, Marti, and Mark, and to all of their wonderful spouses and offspring, I am grateful for so many chances in which to practice what is contained in these pages. As for my wife, Linda, who has supported me in so many ways, it would be difficult to imagine my life without her encouragement, candor, and discipline. I must also thank our sons, Jeremy and Matthew, who have taught me about life and what it means to be a self-reflective, constantly failing, imperfect, but nonetheless optimistic dad. And, finally, I wish to thank our dog, Pyrrho, for teaching me more about myself in a single gesture than all the books on moral philosophy combined. To paraphrase a meme, May I one day become the man Pyrrho thinks I am.

Introduction

*T*his is the fourth book I have written on the topic of critical thinking, and in each book, I always cover the same series of tools that make up what we might call the critical thinking skill set. I have often wondered why, over the past twenty-five years of my academic career, has critical thinking not been in the curricula of all of the primary and secondary education systems. It has been a great mistake in the education systems of our youth to believe that all our students come prepared with the abilities of knowing *how* to think. They don't. At least, most of them don't. So it becomes incumbent on all educators to take the necessary steps to ensure that all students at all levels of education receive a proper education in *how* to think about various subjects and important issues. This means that we must teach critical thinking skills at every level of education—from preschool to graduate school.

Perhaps some of the reasons that such critical thinking skills are not taught at these levels lie in the very terms that are used within the critical thinking skill set. For example, the very name *critical thinking* suggests that it involves a type of negative or critical attack on a person's ideas or beliefs. Who wants to have their ideas criticized or challenged, right? Although it is true that with critical thinking we need to be able to critique all information, this needs to be seen, understood, and accepted as a very positive thing. Unfortunately, we cannot sugarcoat the field of critical thinking by calling it something else. We could try calling it "clear thinking," "helpful-suggestion thinking," or "rainbows and unicorn thinking," but the fact of the matter is that, in order to become intellectually mature, we have to be prepared to accept criticism of our ideas no matter how much we cherish them or have emotionally invested in them.

Another word that might be considered problematic within the field of critical thinking is the use of the term *argument*. The very basis of critical thinking requires us to put our ideas into the form of arguments. But the word *argument* itself is often perceived as having negative connotations, suggesting that people are embroiled in emotionally heated disagreements, and so some might equate the word *argument* to the act of "arguing." This is unfortunate, for, as we shall soon see, putting one's ideas into the forms of arguments is the best possible way to be understood, so there is nothing negative about the use of the word *argument* in critical thinking.

It is even possible that another common term used in the critical thinking skill set has people confused or uncertain, and that is the use of the term *fallacy*. For the record, a fallacy is not a penis; it's an error in reasoning. Although it might sound like the word *phallus*, I can assure you that a fallacy has very little to do with male genitalia.

Critical thinking skills teach us that there really are better and worse ways to think about things. It really is possible to have intelligent discussions, disagree entirely, and still be able to get along. Due to recent events in the world of politics and the media, the *Oxford Dictionary*'s Word of the Year for 2016 was *post-truth*—an adjective defined as "relating to or denoting circumstances in which objective facts are less influential in shaping public opinion than appeals to emotion and personal belief."[1] This is an extremely sad commentary on how information is delivered, interpreted, and acted on. By repeatedly stating talking points—even if they involved false information—politicians are saying whatever they *feel* is appropriate to make their point. This is done through the excessive use of "echo chambers"—a media term indicating the uncritical way in which unchecked and untrue information can be repeatedly stated over and over again until it appears to be factual. In many cases, the false information—sometimes referred to as "alternative facts"[2]—is treated as factual by some news agencies. This is hauntingly similar to what Joseph Goebbels, the Reich minister of propaganda for the Nazis, said during World War II:

> If you tell a lie big enough and keep repeating it, people will eventually come to believe it. The lie can be maintained only for such time as the State can shield the people from the political, economic and/

or military consequences of the lie. It thus becomes vitally important for the State to use all of its powers to repress dissent, for the truth is the mortal enemy of the lie, and thus by extension, the truth is the greatest enemy of the State.[3]

Once "fake news" or "alternative facts" become accepted as factual, it feeds on confirmation bias and becomes entrenched in the minds of people who *want* to believe it to be true. There is supporting evidence indicating that fake news leads to false memories.[4] And when the false memories are accepted as true, they can become so entrenched that it is almost impossible to correct. However, in attempting to respond to and correct the falsities, those who wish to fact-check such claims often come under attack as belonging to a grand conspiracy, trying to suppress the truth. Post-truth politics makes considerable use of conspiracy theories. A recent study suggests that conspiracy theorists actively seek out online communities to continuously reconfirm their biases toward a specific conspiracy theory.[5] To criticize such conspiracy theories with inconvenient things like facts might lead to accusations of being a member of the "mainstream media" or the "Establishment." In critical thinking, this is called "insulating one's argument against criticism." It is an attempt to make any claim impervious to scrutiny and criticism. We will have none of that in this book and, it is hoped, in society. In order to live in free and just societies, all information is open to criticism and scrutiny without exception. So it's time to make facts and critical thinking sexy again.

It has unfortunately become quite fashionable today to claim that what people *feel* about issues should be taken as seriously as the facts about those issues. As we shall see, emotional attachment to specific viewpoints and the facts about the world are often two completely different things. It's not as though a person's feelings are not to be validated; they are. However, one's feelings should be validated only up to the point where they conflict with the facts.

Learning the tools of the critical thinking skill set will allow you to more effectively communicate *what* it is you believe and *why* it is you believe it so that people will have an easier time understanding you. In so doing, you will be empowered with the capacity to better understand what people are saying to you and to know the various components of why and what it is they are saying. Your thinking will become better as well because what emerges from your ability to understand and use these skills is an element of diplomacy and fairness when having intelligent discussions and dialogue about important issues. And this will translate into more civil disagreement.

The biggest takeaway from this book is that if people use the critical thinking skill set *fairly*, they will be more empowered to have meaningful discussions about important issues, disagree entirely, and still be able to get along. Learning these skills will allow us to value discourse over hatred, dialogue over violence, and, most important, fairness and understanding in our disagreements on important issues.

The concept of *fairness* is the *Golden Rule of dialogue* and the *cornerstone of critical thinking.*

If we play fairly and if the others with whom we disagree play fairly, I will guarantee you that both sides will get the most of what they want. But—and this is a very big *but*—both sides *must* play fairly for this to work. If this were done more often, it would save untold amounts of time, energy, and money. But we can be greedy, self-centered, and stupid, and in so doing decide not to play fairly. There are few values we humans hold dearer than fairness. We have built-in, hardwired fairness detectors within us. As such, when it comes to decisions and judgments, we tend to dispute results less if we believe that they were at least arrived at in a fair and just manner. So if we can be fair even when disagreeing, it will increase our capacity to understand and deal with differences of opinions. In a world where disagreements are going to happen, we need to relearn how to have important discussions that may become emotionally heated but also realize that we can and should still get along. It's *easy* to agree and get along, but we have forgotten how to value and use the art of disagreement in civil and political discourse. It is important for us to know that it's *okay* to disagree. We need to accept that we're not always going to agree and that even if we are diametrically opposed to another's viewpoints, we can still be their neighbor, friend, in-law, coworker, or family member.

You believe climate change is real; she doesn't. You believe the Democratic political philosophy is superior; he thinks the Republicans know better. You like the Yankees; she's a Red Sox fan. You're pro-life; she's pro-choice. You say, "To-mah-to"; she says, "Shut the —— up!"[6]

The biggest takeaway here is that we need to relearn *how* to think so that we can disagree and still get along, and this requires maturity and diplomacy, but, above all else, it requires *fairness*. These are not easy traits to develop. In fact, developing and practicing them is one of the toughest challenges we face as inhabitants of a civilized world. Thankfully, the skills of critical thinking provide us with the capacity to be mature, diplomatic, and fair and allow us to disagree in a civil manner. For the majority of us, developing such skills will not happen overnight or in a week or a month. It is something that is ongoing and requires continuous practice, development, and use. But this takes time and a lot of practice, and in today's Age of Immediacy, with information and opinion just a click away, there seems to be less and less time in which to practice such skills. Perhaps this is one of the reasons so many people are feeling their way through issues rather than thinking critically about them.

I
THE ABCS OF CRITICAL THINKING

• 1 •

Why an Argument Is Like a House

*I*n this chapter, we will consider various aspects of argumentation. First, we will consider what an argument is and why it is a good thing to develop when having any kind of discussion. More often than not, people think that arguments are bad things. This is because we often attribute and associate negative value and bitterness when we hear people "arguing." So when we read or hear the word *argument*, it is not surprising that in the minds of many people, it can contain negative connotations. However, quite the contrary is the case. Arguments allow us to construct our ideas in a way that makes it easier for people to understand us. We will also look at different types of reasoning that are used in the development of arguments. For example, we will look at deductive, inductive, and abductive forms of reasoning that help us construct arguments.

WHY AN ARGUMENT IS LIKE A HOUSE

An argument is a good thing. As mentioned above, when we hear the word *argument*, we often attribute negative associations to it because it calls to mind angry, bitter, and sometimes violent altercations both verbally and physically between two or more people. So, just as the term *critical thinking* is off-putting to many people because they expect its users to "criticize" their views to the point of ridicule or embarrassment, so too are negative connotations associated with the term *argument*. It follows, then, that the first hurdle we must overcome in learning how to think critically involves destigmatizing the very language we must use in order to express ourselves more clearly and effectively. So let me assure you that critical thinking is a wonderful skill for anyone and everyone to have and to use. For it is not focused simply on destructively criticizing the arguments or beliefs of others. It is used equally as much in the constructive development of ideas in order to gain greater clarity and understanding. This is a good thing for both sides of an argument.

So what is an argument? An argument is formed when a person makes a claim that is further supported by another statement. For example, when I state, "I believe Justin Bieber is the greatest pop star of all time," I am making a claim. However, this claim by itself is not an argument. It requires further support from at least one other statement. For example, I might believe Justin Bieber is the greatest pop star of all time because of his magnificent singing voice. If that were the case, then I would have an argument. My main point, or *conclusion*, is that Justin Bieber is the greatest pop star of all time. My supporting reason for believing this, or my *premise*, is that he has a magnificent singing voice. So my argument looks like this:

> Justin Bieber is the greatest pop star of all time because of his magnificent singing voice.

Now, whether or not this is a good argument or whether or not you agree with this argument is not the point. The point is that I now have an argument, whereas before I simply had a statement. And my argument, just like all arguments, is *always* made up of two parts: my main point, or what is formally called the conclusion, and my reasons for believing my main point, or what are formally called premises. If you want to be better understood, then you need to put your ideas into the form of arguments. Likewise, if you want to better understand what someone means, try to understand their ideas in the form of arguments.

An argument is essentially the way in which we put together or structure our ideas, beliefs, or opinions so that we are more clearly understood. So the structure of every argument takes the following form:

> Premise(s) + Conclusion = Argument

You now know what an overwhelmingly large part of the world's population does not: the structure of an argument. If any journalist were to walk down any Main Street of any major city in the world with a camera and a microphone and asked people what an argument is, very few would know what you now know. What you now know is that when you put your beliefs, your ideas, and your thoughts into the form of an argument, it greatly increases the likelihood that people will understand what you believe and why you believe it. This, in turn, opens the door for a greater likelihood of being understood. This will then lead to a greater likelihood of more interesting, productive, and relevant discussions about any issue, from the most mundane to the most sublime. It is often the case that people get into heated disputes because they are simply talking past each other and discussing issues emotionally rather than logically. That is to be understood. Very few schools in the world, from kindergarten to grade 12, teach students *how* to think. The skill of thinking is simply assumed in most education systems throughout the world. So it is not surprising to find that when we look to our politicians, our statesmen, and our world leaders to demonstrate effectiveness of thinking and clarity of thought, we are often surprised. But it should come as no surprise for those who have seen the erosion of education systems for many decades. So it is time to make critical thinking sexy again. Once we see the value in effective communication and productive dialogue, the skill set of critical thinking will sell itself. But we have a long way to go, so let's get back to it.

At this point, we don't have to worry too much about whether we agree with the content of the argument; we'll get to that later. Right now, the most important point is to stay focused on the structure of an argument.

So how is an argument like a house? First, recall that the main point you want to express is called the conclusion of an argument. That's like the *roof* of a house. And if you can remember that the supporting statements for your conclusion are called premises, they are like the *walls* that support the roof of the house. But the premises supporting a conclusion, like the walls of a house, will support the roof only if they are firmly anchored onto a strong *foundation*. In critical thinking, the foundation is made up of universal criteria.

So, how well the premises satisfy or fail to satisfy the universal criteria determines the extent to which the structure of an argument is sound or solidly supported. So we literally build arguments in ways similar to the construction of houses. Just as you would never build a structure on an impermanent or questionable foundation—like

Figure 1.1. Argument as House

sand—so too would you avoid developing an argument that could not stand or satisfy universal criteria of acceptability.

Your roof (conclusion) may be a relatively innocuous claim: "It is a lovely day today." Or it could be more controversial: "Elvis was abducted by aliens." But there is a general rule in critical thinking: the greater the conclusion (roof), the stronger the premises (walls) need to be. All houses (as arguments) must rest on the same foundations (universal criteria). However, not all arguments abide by these criteria as well as others. So their premises (walls) become weakened and prone to imbalance. If premises can be demonstrated to be weak in some respects, the house (argument) becomes increasingly prone to collapse.

Not all of our arguments will be able to withstand scrutiny. This is simply a fact of life. For those of you who thought you had good reasons or premises to believe that the Tooth Fairy existed and then found out she didn't, do you still believe in her? Of course not. Your conclusion could not withstand the scrutiny of critical thinking. But that's okay.

Many of our beliefs come under similar scrutiny and must suffer the same fate. If we are wise, we emerge from the rubble of these fallen houses with the renewed ambition to start building new houses with stronger walls.

Just as old dwellings and buildings eventually age, decay, and become uninhabitable, so too do some of our most cherished beliefs. We may think one way in our youth, but eventually, as we age over time, we may come to see the world in vastly different ways. As we

Figure 1.2.   Weak Argument

progress through our landscape of beliefs, we inevitably tear down old and weathered ideas to clear the ground for the construction of new and more soundly built arguments.

THE FOUNDATION OF AN ARGUMENT CONSISTS OF UNIVERSAL CRITERIA

In order for an argument to be solid and sound, not only must the walls be sturdy, but the foundation must provide the greatest support. There are several universal criteria that make up the foundation. These are consistency, simplicity, relevance, reliability, and sufficiency. In critical thinking, criteria are really just standards of judgment that we use for evaluating or testing our claims and those of others. Fortunately, there is universal agreement about the criteria used to support our premises that effectively and efficiently allows us to speak to one another on a very level playing field. Let's look at the first and most important of our universal foundational criteria: consistency.

THE MOTHER OF ALL UNIVERSAL FOUNDATIONAL CRITERIA: CONSISTENCY

There is little doubt that the most important of all universal criteria in critical thinking is *consistency*. So we are going to have to spend a bit of time learning about it. If an argument is not consistent, it is weak and extremely prone to collapse. Consistency is so important that it is sometimes referred to as the "mother of all criteria" and the guiding principle of all rational behavior. Aside from a few world leaders, can you think of a time when *anyone* was ever praised—either in speech or in action (think "alternate facts")—for their inconsistencies? We tend to dislike inconsistencies because we understand the world best when we can predict (with some accuracy) the anticipated outcomes of actions. When our expectations are violated, we experience a sense of dissonance and identify (on a very pragmatic level) the negative aspects and consequences of such inconsistencies. There is overwhelming evidence to support the conclusion that all species highly value consistency in communication and behavior.[1] This is what I believe to be one of the main reasons why humans and other species universally place so much value on the criterion of consistency. Recognizing and utilizing that future events will be similar to past events involves inductive and comparative reasoning, and it has been hardwired into our DNA for hundreds of thousands of years. Because if our beliefs and actions are inconsistent with the way the world actually works, it often has very drastic and harmful effects. And nature can be very cruel in reminding us of the importance of consistency.

I can remember a time when I was teaching at the University of Guelph in Ontario, Canada, and there was a story in the student newspaper about a group visiting the campus who claimed to be able to live off of nothing but oxygen and light—they are called Breatharians. When they came to campus, I went to their display booth in the central student building and questioned them regarding the consistency of their claims. I soon realized that the quickest way to demonstrate the falsity of their claims involved a consistency challenge: I agreed to voluntarily give up my office for several of them to reside in for two weeks without food or water of any kind; however, they could breathe all of the air and leave my lights on all they wanted or even bring in their own special lights. Since it is very difficult for the human body to survive without liquid—even for a relatively short period of time—it should become apparent fairly early on in this challenge that nature would clearly demonstrate the inconsistency of their beliefs. The purpose of such a challenge is not to be vicious, malicious, or otherwise cruel. The forcefulness of the challenge is used to demonstrate the importance of consistency in how we perceive and understand the world. Since it is inconsistent to claim that a person could live on nothing but light and water for two weeks, one needs to consider how the inconsistency of such a claim could be demonstrated. In other words, how else might we falsify such a claim than through empirical demonstration? As it turns out, such a challenge eventually was taken up by the leader of the Breatharians— Jasmuheen, formerly Ellen Greve on Australia's *60 Minutes*:

> Jasmuheen volunteered to appear on Australia's "60 Minutes" to prove her claims of living on light. After 48 hours, her blood pressure increased and she exhibited signs of dehydration. She attributed these symptoms to polluted air. The program moved her to a location further from the city, but as her speech slowed, pupils dilated and weight loss continued, the doctor supervising the observation advised the program to quit the experiment before she lost more kidney function, and they did so. Jasmuheen maintains that "60 Minutes" stopped the test because "they feared [she] would be successful."[2]

Notice how even in the face of such obvious falsifying measures, Jasmuheen still maintains that it is not her beliefs that are factually wrong but rather the fear of the press (and the rest of the world) that she is correct. Such a challenge clearly demonstrates the power of critical thinking and the importance of consistency.

Now if we really want to look at the *facts* regarding Jasmuheen's claim rather than her ideological *feelings*, here they are:

> What happens to the human body without food and water? Without food, the body must find another way to maintain glucose levels. At first, it breaks down glycogen. Then, it turns to proteins and fats. The liver turns fatty acids into by-products called ketone bodies until there are too many of them to process. Then, the body goes into a life-threatening chemical imbalance called ketosis. It's actually dehydration, though, that has a more immediate fatal effect. A person can only survive without water for a matter of days, perhaps two weeks at most. The exact amount of time depends on the outside temperature and a person's characteristics. First, the body loses water through urine and sweat. A person then develops ketosis and uremia, a buildup of toxins in the blood. Eventually, the organ systems begin to fail. The body develops kidney failure, and an

electrolyte imbalance causes cardiac arrhythmia. Dehydration leads to seizures, permanent brain damage or even death. Jasmuheen has said, "If a person is unprepared and not listening to their inner voice there can be many problems with the 21 day [fasting] process, from extreme weight loss to even loss of their life." Science says that the human body cannot survive without food and water for that amount of time, regardless of what the inner voice says.[3]

Notice again how Jasmuheen tried to insulate her beliefs by blaming failure on the individuals themselves rather than on her health advice. So if an individual is unprepared by not listening to their inner voice, this is what causes health problems and even death, not facts like starvation and, far more likely, dehydration. We must remain vigilant in keeping the onus of proof squarely where it rests: with those who make such extraordinary claims. Jasmuheen's attempts to heap excuse after excuse on her failed belief system commits what is known as the ad hoc fallacy (a fallacy we will look at more closely in chapter 6). Basically, the fallacy is committed when people refuse to admit when their belief, opinion, or idea has been demonstrated to be false through empirical or scientific means. Instead of admitting to the obvious inconsistencies of their position, they continue to come up with more rationalizations in defense of it.

If you have ever been bothered watching a political figure discuss important issues only to be shown how, at another time, video footage demonstrates that he or she said exactly the opposite and wondered why this bothered you so much, you're not alone. What you're feeling is a violation of consistency. We humans, along with a lot of other species, are hardwired to detect inconsistencies. Otherwise, our ancestors never would have survived to the point of allowing you to read this book. Without consistency in our lives and minds, we would live in a horrifically mad world that did not make sense. So when the world feels a little out of sorts to you, you can blame your consistency meter that dwells deep inside of you. This is why it is the most important universal foundational criterion on which we measure the value of our beliefs. For if our ideas are inconsistent from the very beginning, they can have no conviction or sway over anyone. Consistency may not guarantee agreement, but it will definitely produce greater clarity of thought.

In today's alternate political universe, with alternative facts, post-truth politics, and glib off-the-cuff comments from all quarters, there is a greater need for clarity of thought, empowerment in presentation of ideas, and directness in communication. People need to know when they're being not only lied to, presented with alternative facts, double-spoken to in a hauntingly similar manner to that found in Orwell's *1984* but also to be able to call some information what it is: bullshit! And they need to be able to understand the nuances and the qualities of such statements in order to hold others accountable for their beliefs and their actions. I find Harry Frankfurt's distinction between "lying" and "bullshit" to be useful in outlining why, specifically, for example, President Trump is so good at pitching it:

> The liar asserts something which he himself believes to be false. He deliberately misrepresents what he takes to be the truth. The bullshitter, on the other hand, is not constrained by any consideration of what may or may not be true. In making his assertion, he is indifferent to whether what he is says is true or false. His goal is not to report facts. It is, rather, to shape the beliefs and attitudes of his listeners in a certain way.[4]

It could be said that Trump comes from a long, highly esteemed line of "bullshitters," and he's not alone in this regard. Let's remember that there are just as many Democratic bullshitters these days as Republicans, and that's because politics, in general, has evolved into a game of ideologies and personal agendas. Bullshitting, of course, dates all the way back to ancient Greece.[5] During these times, there were a group of philosophers known as the Sophists. The Sophists would travel from town to town, and for entertainment, they would engage in formal debates on practically any topic or subject. It was often considered the Sophists' calling card that they would brag about how they could argue the worst case and make it appear more convincing. They were well versed in *rhetoric*, or the ability to convince somebody of their argument. Rhetoric, or what could also be called the art of persuasion, is important. However, right now, I want to stay focused on the importance of universal foundational criteria and why these act as the basis for what determines an argument to be either good or bad.

Now the Sophists, from which we get terms like *sophistry*,[6] were extremely adept at tapping into whatever was necessary in order to win the most votes in a debate. If this meant appealing to the crowd's emotions, so be it. If this meant using pretzel logic or reasoning so twisted that people could not tell whether it was true, so be it. Fortunately for us, perhaps the greatest philosopher of all time, Aristotle, wasn't impressed with this type of bad reasoning. So he developed some basic rules of thinking that would challenge and falsify the claims of the Sophists.

Aristotle decided there had to be a foundational logic that could cut through this kind of bamboozery and hucksterism that defied consistency and fooled audiences. So he developed some basic principles of classical logic known as the *three laws of thought*. As you will see in the next three sections, each law provides the basis for the power and effectiveness of the criterion of consistency.

The Law of Identity

This is the first and most basic law. It states that $x = x$, where x refers in both cases to the same thing at the same time and in the same respect. The truth of this law becomes obvious whenever someone tries to make statements such as "A toothbrush is not a toothbrush" or "A great white shark is a Lazy Boy recliner." Violating such a law immediately reveals an inconsistency. So if you happen to be swimming in the ocean and you come across a great white shark, don't try to sit or lie down on it.[7]

Here are some proper examples of the law of identity:

212°F	=	100°C
Iceland has witnessed peace for over 50 years	=	Iceland has not been at war for over half a century
If you don't eat your meat you can't have any pudding!	=	How can you have any pudding if you don't eat your meat?[1]
This	=	This[2]

1. Pink Floyd, "Another Brick in the Wall," from the album *The Wall*.
2. Robert De Niro, *The Deer Hunter*.

This law provides a basis for us to understand what things are by what defines them as well as how they are distinguished from everything else. In other words, my computer is not my dog, my dog is not my office door, my office door is not my car, and my car is not my son. Each of these things has unique identities, and we come to know these things through their many properties. To show the absurdity of the results of contradicting this law, imagine a world in which people, statements, and objects randomly changed properties and functions; for example, if you tried to open your car door and it turned into a hippopotamus, if on some days water satisfied thirst but on other days it did not, or if the laws of physics worked only randomly and unpredictably, neither you nor anyone else nor any other species on this planet would be able to predict and exercise any type of control over their environments. In such a bizarre world where everything and its opposite can happen, we can only imagine the absolute horror that would ensue in trying to survive and adapt to such surreal circumstances.

The Law of Noncontradiction

The second law that Aristotle developed to demonstrate the importance of consistency maintains that either a state of being or a statement and its negation cannot both be true. In other words, it is impossible—both logically and physically—for an object to be entirely liquid and entirely solid at the same time and in the same respect. It is impossible for me to say that I am now both lying and not lying at the same time and in the same respect. In the same manner, we can also say that a statement cannot both be true and false simultaneously. For example, the statement "The Buffalo Bills both won Super Bowl XXV and lost it" is a contradictory statement and cannot be true. The law is basically saying, "You can't have your cake and eat it too." You can have your cake, or you can eat it, but you can't have it both ways. That's all there is to it. I remember coming through a car wash near my home. At the point of exit, there is a traffic light that has an amber light that says, "Wait" and a green light that says, "Go." The last few times I came through the car wash, both lights were flashing simultaneously.

Such situations can be confusing (and potentially dangerous) because we are given contradictory commands. Arguments cannot be consistent if parts of them are contradictory.

The Law of Excluded Middle

With this particular law, Aristotle said that any meaningful claim that one thinks or any natural state of being must be either true or false. In other words, there is literally no middle ground. For example, it must be either true or false that you can run a mile in less than two minutes.

Figure 1.3.   Contradictory Instructions

There is no middle ground allowed in this distinction; either you can do it, or you can't. Another way of understanding the lack of middle ground is to see this law as being binary. Like the 0s and 1s in computer code, this law is disjunctive in stating that either something is true or it is not. The idea that there is no such thing as being "a little pregnant" demonstrates this law quite well.

So, when taken together, the law of identity, the law of noncontradiction, and the law of excluded middle provide the basis for the universal foundational criterion of *consistency*. We use these three laws of thought in everyday discussions involving the most mundane considerations to the most sublime ponderings. Consistency is the cornerstone of the foundation of universal criteria because once it is violated, once we discover that an argument's premises are inconsistent, there is no further need for discussion or dialogue until the inconsistency is recognized, accepted, and corrected.

These three laws are considered the foundations of rational thought because they disallow people from stating unaccountable inconsistencies and contradictions. So, for example, when the newly inaugurated president of the United States, Donald Trump, boldly proclaimed that the pictures of crowds at his inauguration were falsified and that there were well over a million supporters in attendance; that God stopped the skies from raining on his inauguration even though his wife was holding an umbrella and other members in the crowd (including past President George W. Bush) were all wearing plastic ponchos because it was raining; and that the skies opened and the sun shone down on him because of God, these all violate the three laws of thought that underlie the criterion of consistency.[8] Yet Trump is such a good marketer that it appears that he believes that by repeating the same claims, people will come to believe them.

One should now be able to see and understand why consistency is the most important universal foundational criterion in support of our premises, which in turn support our conclusion. For example, during the Senate confirmation hearing of Judge Brett Kavanaugh in 2018, President Trump said that Christine Blasey Ford's testimony was credible and believable, calling her "a very credible witness." A few nights later while at a rally in Mississippi, Trump began to belittle and ridicule Blasey Ford's testimony:

> "How did you get home? 'I don't remember,'" Trump said at the rally Tuesday in Southaven. "How did you get there? 'I don't remember,' Where is the place? 'I don't remember,' How many years ago was it? 'I don't know. I don't know. I don't know.'" Imitating Ford, he added, "But I had one beer—that's the only thing I remember."[9]

So again we see yet another example of blatant inconsistency. Such inconsistencies strike at the very heart of what it means to think and act responsibly and undermine logic, hence the need to learn the basic skill set of critical thinking. We need to learn or relearn *how* to think, for in learning *how* to think critically and responsibly, we empower ourselves and those with whom we associate with the ability to recognize and call out bullshit whenever we encounter it.

The reason that facts are important, evidence is important, and establishing the truth is important is because it holds people accountable who try to use pretzel logic and biased rhetoric in an attempt to circumvent the three laws of thought, which provide the foundational appeal of consistency to our statements. Without these laws of thought, anything goes. Such a world is far too unsettling, disturbing, and dangerous for us to allow this to happen. It is for these reasons (and more) that *consistency* is the most important of all criteria when it comes to supporting premises.

TYPES OF CONSISTENCY

When it comes to consistency, there are two types: internal and external. If a person's ideas, beliefs, or opinions possess *internal consistency*, then it means that they are related to one another and, relative to the set of premises, commit no errors with regard to either of the three laws of thought. In other words, internal consistency refers to the way in which one's premises are related to and consistent with each other *within* a particular belief system. However, there are plenty of arguments, beliefs, and opinions that can be internally consistent.

For example, it is easy to display spectacular internal consistency that demonstrates why I believe that the reason my socks go missing out of my clothes dryer is actually due to mischievous elves. If you try to falsify my claim by setting up video cameras, I will tell you that they are invisible. When you set up a web-like array of laser detectors, I tell you that they do not possess mass. You may try to falsify my claim by spreading flour on the ground around the dryer so that we can see evidence of where the elves have walked, but I tell you they can fly and hover. And because of all of these traits, I can demonstrate the internal consistency of why my socks seem to go missing from my dryer. So, no matter how much you try to falsify my belief, I can always come up with disprovable responses to any scrutiny and maintain the internal consistency of my belief in mischievous, invisible, flying elves.

Although this argument may seem internally consistent, the conclusion I have provided—that elves steal socks out of my dryer—and the premises I use to support this conclusion, that is, that they are invisible, possess no mass, and can fly and hover, do not possess any *external consistency* with the natural world and our understanding of it. In the attempt to confirm such a claim, we might set up traps, motion-detecting sensors, and video surveillance cameras to provide the empirical evidence and proof required for people to believe that such things as mischievous elves truly exist. However, when no such evidence turns up, what are we to believe? The lack of evidence has failed to confirm such a conclusion. This then leads us to maintain that, although internally consistent to the believer in invisible, massless, flying elves, this argument bears no *external* consistency with the natural world. And until such a time that the claimant can demonstrate the existence of such beings—that is, demonstrate external consistency with the natural world—we have no good reason to believe him. So, without supporting evidence that leads me to conclude that invisible mischievous elves really exist in the natural world, I am not compelled in any way to believe such an argument.

The same applies to the case of the Breatharians—that is, their belief system maintains a type of *internal consistency*. And this is because within their group, there are no fact-checkers around to confirm or falsify their successes other than themselves, and any failures reported to the public will be the result of the individuals themselves rather than the system itself. This type of internal consistency is extremely dangerous because it is insulated against counterfactuals, or any attempts to falsify the set of beliefs. It is only when we start to look for *external consistency*, that is, consistency between beliefs and scientific facts of the natural world, that we see the breakdown of such a particular set of beliefs. Unfortunately, the external consistency of the Breatharian philosophy led to the deaths of at least three people and countless others who became seriously ill.

One of the quickest ways to spot inconsistency is to identify contradictions. For example, whenever someone makes a universal claim—whether affirmative (e.g., "I always do ———") or negative (e.g., "I never do ———"), you can demonstrate inconsistency in his or her claims by providing just one counterfactual incident. Think of how many people throughout history have stood for specific values and principles—like truth, justice, freedom, and dignity—only to be discovered to violate these principles. And think of how many times communities have been shocked to discover the inconsistent behavior of their politicians, physicians, priests, coaches, bosses, teachers, and so on. If our premises are not consistent, they will not be valued, and our house cannot stand and will collapse.

Let's now turn our attention to the four remaining universal criteria that collectively act as foundations on which to anchor our premises.

Simplicity

Sometimes referred to as parsimony, simplicity is universally valued as a criterion to support premises because if we can present an argument that accomplishes just as much but with fewer premises, it tends to be more highly valued. Often referred to as Occam's razor—named after William of Occam, a fourteenth-century Franciscan friar and Scholastic philosopher—the criterion is often best summed up in his famous saying: "Do not multiply entities beyond necessity."[10] What Occam meant by this is that you really don't need more premises than are necessary to responsibly support your conclusion and satisfy the foundational criteria. One might even say that Occam was the originator of the KISS principle (Keep It Simple Stupid). In other words, when faced with competing arguments, the one that can say more with the fewest premises is generally favored. For example, when Jamal Khashoggi was murdered in the Saudi Arabian consulate on October 2, 2018, in Istanbul, Turkey, the government of Saudi Arabia continuously provided misleading and erroneous reasons for Khashoggi's disappearance. As we now know, the simplest explanation—that he was targeted for assassination—turns out be the correct explanation. Generally, it just makes more sense for us to believe that a less complicated and more precise manner for providing evidence of a conclusion is better than a drawn-out and complicated one. To return to one of our previous examples, in the case of missing socks from the clothes dryer, it is a far simpler explanation to argue that they are missing due to human carelessness or by accident than to argue for the existence of invisible, massless, flying, mischievous elves. Although a less complicated argument is not always best—because some ideas require extremely complex arguments—for the purposes of practicality and efficiency, the criterion of simplicity is universally valued and accepted.

Reliability

The manner in which information is attained and used as premises to support a conclusion is extremely important. Attaining dependable, factual information is critical in the continued support of one's conclusion. Reliability is a universal criterion that demands that we attain our information from trustworthy sources and that we do not shirk our responsibility in this regard. Many people around the world formulate opinions about extremely important issues based on information they find on Facebook or Twitter. We now know that such social media platforms are filled with false information from various sources in an attempt to sway public opinion. Not only has there been overwhelming evidence of such activity from Russia and China, but places like Myanmar have done so to horrendous effect. The spreading of false information of Rohingya Muslims by Buddhist extremists (yes, even Buddhists have their extremists) has led to an enormous campaign of ethnic cleansing, causing hundreds of thousands of refugees to flee into neighboring Myanmar. The problem with such sources of information is that it is very easy to present "fake news." As we saw earlier in this chapter, if you tell a lie often enough, it will become accepted as the truth. Reliability of shared information is essential, and that is why teachers and journalists generally hold such important roles in society. If the information the public receives has not been attained in a responsible and reliable manner, then we the people suffer because we are not making *informed* opinions or decisions about that information.

In many respects, it is the responsibility of the media to prevent the reporting of "alternative facts" from ever happening. However, over the past several years, the media seem as though they cannot get enough of President Trump and what they call his hucksterism. So now the world has seen what can happen when a perfect storm of eventualities occurs, that is, when the media meet a person who they consider is one who is attempting to undermine democratic values.

The past few years have revealed to the entire world what can happen when emotions take precedence over reason and reflection. In other words, the limbic systems of enough people often win out over the prefrontal cortexes of those in opposition. Democracy and the media must guard against focusing too much on what people *feel* about issues and not take these as seriously as the *facts* about issues. Emotions and facts can often run counter to one another. And if we wish to preserve our democratic values, it is the job of the media and educators to keep facts and feelings as far apart as possible.

It follows that reliability and media literacy go hand in hand. The more literate one becomes in terms of reliable media sources, the greater the likelihood of stronger premises supporting a conclusion. Conversely, the more gullible one is in accepting information from dubious and unreliable sources, the greater the likelihood for weaker premises—and the eventual collapse of one's argument. The same holds true for the information provided by professionals within given fields. For example, an ultrasound will provide more reliable information about the development of a fetus than that provided by a psychic. A qualified physician will be more reliable in telling you about the importance of vaccinations than a famous model/actress/activist. And a certified, licensed garage mechanic will be more reliable in telling you information about your car than an unqualified athlete. So it follows, then, that if it can be demonstrated that the premises of an argument have not been attained from reliable sources, it becomes quite easy to demonstrate their weakness and topple the argument (house).

Relevance

It seems blatantly obvious that premises should be relevant to the support of a conclusion. Yet there are many ways in which people introduce irrelevant premises into an argument in the guise of presenting relevant points. A fallacy called a *red herring* is a fallacy of improper relevance (something we will look at in more detail in chapter 6). One commits a red herring fallacy when one attempts to circumvent addressing or responding to the topic at hand by discussing a subject or subjects that have nothing to do with the currently discussed topic. Many red herring fallacies have been committed throughout history. For example, during the September 27, 2016, presidential debate, when asked how he was going to cut taxes for the wealthy, candidate Trump said, "Well, I'm really calling for major jobs, because the wealthy are going to cause tremendous jobs." This has nothing to do with the question/topic at hand; that is, how is Trump going to cut taxes for the wealthy? Therefore, it does not satisfy the foundational criterion of relevance. But to pick on a Democrat for a minute, when asked specifically about her tax-increase proposals, Hillary Clinton criticized Trump's ideas rather than stipulate, specifically, what her own plan was to address this issue. And in the fall of 2018, during a U.S. Senate hearing investigating sexual assault allegations, the following tense dialogue took place between Minnesota Senator Amy Klobuchar and then Supreme Court justice candidate Brett Kavanaugh:

KLOBUCHAR: "Was there ever a time when you drank so much that you couldn't remember what happened or part of what happened the night before?"

KAVANAUGH: "No. I remember what happened and I think you've probably had beers, Senator."

When asked the question again, Judge Kavanaugh responded by asking the senator, "I'm curious if you have [blacked out from drinking too much]."

So, instead of answering the question directly and honestly, Kavanaugh committed a red herring by avoiding commenting on the topic at hand. He deflected the focus away from his consideration of blacking out from alcohol consumption to the very person who is asking him the question. What the tools of critical thinking provide us with is an understanding that Kavanaugh's response to Senator Klobuchar's question is rendered irrelevant because it literally has nothing to do with the topic at hand. So, in Kavanaugh's case, what does the fact that Senator Klobuchar may or may not have drunk to a point where she blacked out have anything to do with Kavanaugh's answer? Nothing; it is completely irrelevant. But let's take this one step further. Even if Kavanaugh's irrelevant question was answered by Klobuchar affirmatively—that is, she has blacked out many times before from excessive drinking—it would not in any way detract from the importance of whether Kavanaugh did so. Klobuchar was not the one under investigation—Kavanaugh was. As such, his elusive and childish red herring responses and bizarre questioning back to Klobuchar have no relevance to the issue at hand whatsoever. Remember, a conclusion should follow from the premises supplied, and if they are relevant, they will provide the conclusion with greater support. When your premises are irrelevant, they don't count for anything, and they'll sometimes make you look silly. So stick to the topic!

Sufficiency

The last foundational universal criterion we need to consider is *sufficiency*. We all have some idea of what it means for something to be sufficient. Sufficiency requires enough of *something* to satisfy some condition, want, goal, and so on. For example, if I am in a busy metropolitan city like Paris and I need to get from one place to another, a taxi would be sufficient. I do not need an armored motorcade with limousine service (as nice as that might be) to get me down the Champs-Élysées.

In critical thinking, we often talk of premises providing the conclusion with *enough* evidence for support. But how much is enough? When are the premises sufficient in providing enough evidence to convince someone of your conclusion? The astronomer Carl Sagan once said, "Extraordinary claims require extraordinary evidence." This means that the larger or more substantial your conclusion is, the more sufficiently convincing the evidence will need to be to support it. For example, if someone were to claim that Bigfoot exists, then what premises would sufficiently support this conclusion? For years, we have seen people claiming to have seen Bigfoot, found his big footprints in snow, heard him, and so on. Many different premises have been offered, but none have been able to satisfy the foundational criterion of sufficiency. That's because no one has ever presented compelling evidence that satisfies this criterion. But there is one very simple way to sufficiently prove Bigfoot's existence: show us a body! If anyone could provide just one body, that's all that needs to be done to sufficiently prove that such a being exists. You would think, with so many sightings, that eventually someone, somewhere, would shoot one of these Sasquatches. Or why hasn't anyone simply stumbled across the corpse of one or its skeletal remains? What about scatology—the biological field of study that examines animal waste. Scatology allows researchers to determine a great deal of information about a creature, such as its diet, living conditions, health, diseases, migratory patterns, and so on. You would think with so many sightings of such a large creature that Bigfoot must take enormous dumps, yet we find no evidence of scatological remains? No shit, literally. So far, there has been nothing but hearsay, bad video footage, ridiculous footprint casts, and legendary tales. So the argument for the existence of Bigfoot fails because it does not present sufficient premises to support such a conclusion. Show me sufficient reason to believe in Bigfoot, and I must follow where the evidence leads. We will look at this topic in more detail in chapter 7, but so far, we can conclude that the evidence does not lead me to believe that such a being exists. Should this change in the future, however, I am always open to the possibility of changing my mind.

The Neutrality of the Universal Foundational Criteria

These five universal criteria—consistency, simplicity, reliability, relevance, and sufficiency—provide the foundational support on which all of our premises rest. If it can be demonstrated that an argument's premises fail to satisfy any (or all) of these criteria, then the argument is doomed to collapse much like a building whose walls cannot support its roof. And it is very important to remember that it does not matter how much one is emotionally attached to an argument. The tools of critical thinking are not concerned with how we *feel* about issues, ideas, opinions, or beliefs. In this respect, these tools are like the principles of mathematics. They are neutral and serve us only when used in accordance to their definitions and intended use.

Now that you know far more than most of the world about what an argument is, how it is structured, and how it must be supported, it is time to consider the types of reasoning that are used in constructing or building arguments like houses, as solid structures.

TYPES OF REASONING

There are several forms, modes, or types of reasoning we use every day to think about things. And they are really just different ways in which we can consider information. Although there are several different types or ways to reason and develop arguments, we are going to consider only the three that are arguably the most important and definitely the most widely used:

1. Deductive reasoning
2. Inductive reasoning
3. Abductive reasoning

Deductive Reasoning: "Elementary, My Dear Watson"[11]

Deductive reasoning is the type of reasoning that readers witness Sherlock Holmes using in solving his crimes in Arthur Conan Doyle's stories of the great detective. Carefully sifting through the evidence surrounding a crime, understanding the *relationship* between the various pieces, and knowing what *must* follow from the evidence—not what *might* follow or *could* follow but *must* follow—leads to an inevitable and definite conclusion as to the identity of the murderer. If you have ever played the board game Clue, you know that, once the identity of the murderer has been determined (through a process of elimination), it clearly *has* to have been *that* particular person, in *that* specific place, with *that* specific weapon—no ifs, ands, or buts about it. For example, *Colonel Mustard* did it in the *ballroom* with a *candlestick*. It's not as though it *may* have been him—it *had* to be him! The process in which the conclusion was reached uses deductive reasoning, whereby the conclusion is certain and irreversible. In other words, the conclusion *must* follow from the premises. Formally, this is referred to as "logical validity."

Here are some examples of logical validity using deductive reasoning:

- If all politicians are liars and Jones is a politician, it must follow that Jones is a liar.
- If all humans are mortal and you are a human, it must follow that you are mortal.
- If you are allergic to tree nuts and had eaten pine nuts, you would have trouble breathing. But you are not having trouble breathing, so it must follow that you have not eaten pine nuts.
- If all fish have cells in their bodies and all cells contain DNA, it must follow that fish have DNA.
- If two people are in an elevator and one of them farts, everyone knows who did it.

It is important to note that, in all of the above examples, the premises do not necessarily have to be true for the argument to be valid. For in each case, their truth is *assumed*. In other words, we assume that *if* the premises are true, the conclusion *has* to follow.

Here's a story that clearly illustrates the assumed truth of premises and the use of deductive reasoning.

Imagine that, in a large midwestern U.S. town, there's a fund-raising dinner in honor of a politician named Donna Grainger. Grainger is running for reelection as senator of a midwestern state, but she is late arriving at the gala dinner. The master of ceremonies is worried and so asks Father Michael Bridgeman—a Catholic priest who was seated at the head table—to get up and talk to the audience until Grainger arrives. He agrees to do so and says the following: "When I was first ordained as a priest, quite a few years ago, I was given the task of hearing confession.[12] You can imagine how shocked I was when my first confessor was a woman who confessed to me that she had poisoned her husband's tea. The poison caused her husband to have a heart attack, and he died. She then confessed to having received $1 million in insurance money for his death!"

At that particular moment, Senator Grainger arrives, and the crowd applauds. Father Bridgeman joins the applause as he returns to his seat. The senator makes her way to the podium. After the applause quiets, she thanks everybody for attending, looks at the head table, and recognizes Father Bridgeman. "Well it certainly is good to see everyone here tonight. Thank you all for coming. I see that Father Bridgeman is here. Father Bridgeman might not realize this, but *I* was his first confessor."

She wonders why an awkward silence falls over the room.

Now, what can we conclude—or, more accurately, deduce—from these premises? Is it that Donna Grainger poisoned her husband's tea, killed him, and collected $1 million in insurance money? You could answer yes, no, or maybe. Given the information we have at this point, the correct answer in this case is maybe. We do not actually have all the facts, so we cannot know for sure if Donna Grainger is a murderer. However, here is how deductive reasoning works. *If* what Father Bridgeman said is true and *if* what Donna Grainger said is true, it *must* follow that she poisoned her husband's tea, causing him to have a heart attack that thereby killed him, and then collected $1 million in insurance money. But notice that the premises *must* be true in order for the conclusion to follow. This is how deductive reasoning works. The conclusion *must* follow from the previous premises. In other words, it cannot be otherwise.

But remember that the conclusion that Donna Grainger is a murderer can follow only *if* what both she and Father Bridgeman said is true. Father Bridgeman could have been mistaken. Perhaps it was his third confessor who confessed to being a murderer and not his first. Or perhaps Grainger was mistaken and was not actually his first confessor. If we investigated further, we could establish Grainger's innocence by discovering that her husband is still alive or that she never married.

Then these findings would immediately exonerate her from the charge of murder. But never forget that with deductive reasoning, *if* what she said is true and *if* what Father Bridgeman said is true, then she *must* be a murderer. Just like in the game of Clue, there can be no other ways about it. The argument would formally look like this:

> Premise 1: Father Bridgeman's first confessor confessed to murdering her husband and collecting $1 million in insurance money.
> Premise 2: Senator Donna Grainger was Father Bridgeman's first confessor.
> Conclusion: Donna Grainger murdered her husband and collected $1 million in insurance money.[13]

Deductive reasoning is a very powerful tool in formulating arguments and understanding the inferences of premises. It relies on pure reason to see connections or relationships between pieces of information. Nobody ever had to have witnessed Donna Grainger physically putting the poison in her husband's tea to discover her guilt. This is because the power of deductive reasoning can put the pieces of the puzzle together in such a way that it would be impossible to conclude otherwise. In this way, such reasoning does not require us to use our physical senses to empirically confirm her actions, only to deduce the conclusion based on sufficient circumstantial evidence.

Inductive Reasoning: "It's Alive!"

When Dr. Frankenstein attracted a lightning bolt to his laboratory in order to provide enough electricity to light the spark of life within his cadaver of creation, he witnessed for himself the startling discovery of bringing life back from the dead. Even though this is entirely a fictional scientific account, we know that he could not have done so without the use of inductive reasoning. Unlike deductive reasoning, the conclusions arrived at using inductive reasoning are not logically valid but are considered to be reasonable, warranted, or probable. And unlike deductive reasoning, which uses pure reason and logic to deduce the conclusion based on a series of premises, inductive reasoning relies heavily on what is called "empirical evidence." This is evidence that is attained through the use of our five senses: sight, sound, taste, hearing, and touch. We just saw that, with deductive reasoning, if the premises are assumed to be true and follow specific forms, then the conclusion must logically follow. With inductive reasoning, human empirical observations through the use of our five senses provide probable conclusions according to statistical generalizations. Consider the following example. If I held a coin between my forefinger and thumb and then opened them over a table, you would watch the coin fall to the table. If I were to do this repeatedly, there would accumulate sufficient statistical instances to warrant the generalization that, under the same circumstances, the next time I opened my fingers, the coin would fall to the table. This is how inductive reasoning works. It is the hallmark of scientific reasoning. It allows us to generalize that future episodes will be similar to past episodes—and not only with things like coins but also with anything possessing mass—like keys, a cell phone, or a wallaby. It is by no means a perfect type of reasoning, but it is nonetheless a very powerful tool in understanding cause-and-effect relationships in the natural world. This type of reasoning has allowed scientists to put people on the moon, cure diseases, circumnavigate the globe, and all and every other manner of scientific discovery.

Abductive Reasoning: The Semmelweis Reflex

Unlike either deductive or inductive reasoning, abductive reasoning is interesting and unique. It is sometimes referred to as "reasoning to the best explanation." What that means is that when there isn't enough evidence to definitively conclude and understand a particular aspect of the world, abductive reasoning is often used to provide a hypothesis that makes sense for now. A historical example should illustrate this type of reasoning quite well. In Vienna, Austria, in the 1840s, there was a physician named Dr. Ignaz Semmelweis. In the hospital at which Dr. Semmelweis worked, women in his ward were dying of what was called "childbed fever"—the actual medical term is puerperal fever. The death rate in his ward was roughly five times higher than in the other wards, where women were tended to by midwives. He was perplexed that this was happening since great care had been taken to ensure that women in his ward would not be afflicted with such a deadly illness.

Here's a bit of a backstory to provide some context. During that time in history, no women were admitted to medical school. The

DR. IGNAZ SEMMELWEIS

Figure 1.4.   Dr. Ignaz Semmelweis

male medical students would first go to anatomy class and then to the various wards to examine patients. After dissecting cadavers, they did not wash their hands, wear gloves, or use any disinfectant whatsoever because no germ theory existed at that time. One day, Semmelweis observed his friend and colleague who had accidentally cut himself with a scalpel while performing an autopsy on a cadaver. A few days later, the man died, exhibiting the exact same symptoms as the women who were dying of childbed fever. Semmelweis realized that there must be something in the cadavers that was being passed along to the women and caused their illness. He hypothesized that such "cadaveric matter" might be too small for the naked eye to see, so he had all of the medical students wash their hands in chlorinated lime before they visited the wards. The number of incidences of childbed fever dropped dramatically. Even though Semmelweis could not see the germs that were causing the illness, he hypothesized that such microscopic agents *must* be the cause of the illness. So he could confirm his hypothesis by using a strong antibacterial cleansing agent. This is how Semmelweis reasoned abductively to the best explanation of the cause of childbed fever.[14] So Semmelweis was able to infer that there was something too small for the naked eye to see (empirical observation) that was causing a deadly human illness. Sadly, history is not without irony. Even though Semmelweis used abductive reasoning to reach a conclusion that saved so many lives, his professional peers scoffed at his germ theory hypothesis and refused to listen to him. He was fired from the hospital and spent his final days attempting to popularize his book *The Etiology, Concept, and Prophylaxis of Childbed Fever*. His professional colleagues rejected his views, and he eventually suffered from depression, forgetfulness, and other neurological complaints (possibly Alzheimer's disease or early-onset dementia). He was admitted to a mental asylum where he was kicked and beaten by staff. His wounds became infected, and he died of sepsis—a similar type of infection that his abductive reasoning helped to cure in so many women. Fortunately, for the rest of humanity, his ideas were eventually taken seriously by scientists such as Louis Pasteur and Joseph Lister and were adopted by the entire medical community. Today, the world owes much to this man and his use of abductive reasoning, which has saved millions of lives.

The premises we use to support our conclusions must satisfy the universal criteria of consistency, simplicity, reliability, relevance, and sufficiency. It is important to remember that an argument takes the form of a house with its conclusion as the roof, its premises as the walls, and the universal criteria as the foundation. When it comes to the types of reasoning used in argumentation, we have considered three types: deduction, induction, and abduction. Each one is important because they provide us with the capacity to more effectively and responsibly build our arguments.

Now that we have considered some of the basic key components of argumentation, we need to turn our attention to the various factors that cause us to see and understand the world differently from one another and that lead to disagreements: *biases*.

· 2 ·

Be Aware of Biases

$\mathcal{I}$n this chapter, we will look at one of the most interesting elements of critical thinking: human biases. No matter who you are, where you were born, or how you were raised, you cannot escape the numerous influences and constraints that have biased your thoughts and your actions throughout your life. A bias is a way in which people are influenced or constrained in the various ways they understand and act on various types of information. The manner in which we eventually come to acquire, revise, and retain opinions, beliefs, and attitudes about issues is the result of a long process of development, influenced by internal and external biases. Even before we were born, there were factors that would influence and bias the way in which we see and understand the world. We now need to become familiar with what these factors are to better understand not only how and why we now believe the things we do but also why we tend to disagree about important issues.

There are many different types of biases, but they all generally fall under two categories: *biological* and *cultural*. Biological biases include factors such as genetic and epigenetic influences, neuropsychological factors, emotions, age, health, and sex. Cultural biases involve constraints and influences such as family upbringing, ethnicity, religion, geographic location, friends, education, and the media. Everything you think and everything you do is the result of your biological and cultural biases. In learning how to think critically, readers are encouraged to be aware of their own biases and conduct a *bias check* to become aware that any new information presented to them must pass through a series of biased filters before they can accept it, reject it, or remain neutral to it. We often favor information that confirms our own biases—appropriately

31

named *confirmation bias*. This is normal, and this is what it means in many respects to be human; that is, in seeking out information that makes us feel knowledgeable, confident, and secure, we need continued validation that what we believe is relevant, truthful, and worthy of being held in belief as a guide to our behavior. In critical thinking, however, we develop the ability to acknowledge and identify what our biases are in an effort to more fairly understand why it is we believe what we do and why it is that we act according to those particular beliefs. In this way, we become more critically reflective of our beliefs and can become fairer in our treatment of others whose opinions, ideas, and beliefs may differ from our own. We first consider the biological influences that bias the way in which we see and understand the world.

BIOLOGICAL BIASES

Genetic Influences

The first biological bias to consider is that which resides in every cell inside our bodies: our deoxyribonucleic acid (DNA). The DNA in every one of our cells codes for particular types of traits and behaviors, just as it does in every other living plant and animal species on the planet. It should come as little surprise, then, that our own genetic makeup will bias us in particular ways. For example, just consider the characteristic traits of homosexuality and attention-deficit/hyperactive disorder (ADHD). If you currently believe that homosexuality is a life choice and has no basis in biology, then you need to explain why homosexuals, throughout the ages, did not simply choose to be heterosexual. Homosexuals have suffered and been oppressed for millennia because of sexual attraction beyond their choosing. So it is very important, when discussing any issues related to homosexuality (such as same-sex marriage) to better understand how sexual orientation is biased in biology. This would, in turn, allow us to treat people more fairly and equitably. But it requires the acknowledgment, understanding, and acceptance of the biological sciences as they relate to human sexuality and apparent decision-making activities. We shall consider this topic in more depth in the final chapter. For now, we need to realize that the same biological constraints that hold true for heterosexual attraction hold true in biasing people to be homosexual. People are biologically biased to be attracted to the opposite sex, the same sex, animals, vegetables, and all manner of inanimate objects. Also—and this is not going to sit well with a lot of people—we need to realize and accept the fact that even pedophiles are biased to be attracted to children. So the biology of human sexuality must act as a basis of information in order for anyone to have reasonable and fair discussions about topics such as same-sex marriage, pedophilia, and so on. People do not simply "choose" one day what their particular sexual preference is going to be. If you have no sexual attraction to children or same-sex partners in any way, does this mean that you can simply "choose" to do so at any point in time? Of course not. Sexual attraction is a hardwired biological bias that makes it extremely difficult to "choose" otherwise. Many gay people throughout history were forced to either "choose" a heterosexual partner to conform to societal norms or carefully hide their true sexuality. For example, throughout recent and ancient history, these included people such as Rock Hudson, Anthony Perkins, Wanda Sykes, Elton John, Little Richard, Alexander the Great, Meredith Baxter, Cole Porter, Pyotr Ilyich Tchaikovsky, Oscar Wilde, Plato, Leonardo da Vinci, Billie Jean King, Michelangelo, and my sixth-grade teacher. And this practice still continues today—not only in intolerant countries like Saudi Arabia, Iran, Iraq, and so on but also in the United States.[1] So we need to grow up as humans and realize that homosexuality is not a life choice and that, as such, it is no different than having blue eyes rather than brown. And we need to understand the basic facts of human sexuality before we begin to have intelligent discussions about it.

A similar type of biological bias holds true for those afflicted with ADHD. Before the development of a genetic understanding of human behavior, young children possessing specific genes for ADHD faced great difficulty and challenges, not to mention ridicule and punishment from their teachers, parents, and others. Just imagine how many children were punished—in so many different ways—for being labeled as "brats" prior to our current understanding of the effects of genetic predispositions. The field of genetics has advanced considerably in the past fifty years. We know far more about the genetic factors that bias someone toward ADHD, and as a result, we are in a much better position to understand how people with this particular bias behave and, in so doing, can more efficiently facilitate an environment in which they may thrive, contribute, and excel.

Epigenetics

We must realize that genes do not work solely in isolation but rather in relation to other genes and environmental factors. The field of epigenetics is advancing in ways that demonstrate how environmental factors play a key role in influencing the ways genes either express or do not express under specific circumstances. Epigenetics literally means "on top of" or "above" genetics. So modifications to DNA occur externally, which either slows or speeds up the process of turning genes on or keeping them suppressed—terms known as *acetylation* and *methylation*. The modifications themselves do not change or alter the DNA sequence. Instead, they affect how cells *read* genes. An analogy for epigenetics that is sometimes used to clarify matters compares a person's DNA to the script of a movie. The lines of the actors would direct conversation within the shooting of the film as genes do within our bodies. However, epigenetics act like the director of the film, and different directors would create different ways in how the movie would appear and play out.[2]

One of the more striking examples of epigenetics involves the use of rodent models. Chronic stress, due to separation from their mothers experienced early in life, has altered not only the adult behavior of mice but also their offspring for several generations. Even though the offspring had not undergone the same stress conditions as their parents or grandparents, they still experience the same depressive and impulsive behaviors and altered social skills. In other words, some of the actions and behavior of your grandparents will influence the speed and frequency with which your genes either express or do not express for particular traits. This particular bias is completely beyond your control and influences us from past generations literally from beyond the grave. This should lead us to consider our own activities, which will ultimately have similar effects on our grandchildren in the future.

Neuropsychological Influences

Our brains control every aspect of our conscious lives. Because brain activity is at the seat of how we process information, we need to seriously consider how this wondrous organ—this three-pound neural mass of electric meat—may bias or influence our behavior. If you have ever known anyone who has suffered from mental illness, you will understand the ways in which they are biased to see the world differently simply because there may be a chemical imbalance within their brains. Psychological disorders such as depression, bipolar disorder, posttraumatic stress disorder (PTSD), obsessive-compulsive disorder (OCD), and schizophrenia can have devastating effects on people and their families. This leads to the obvious conclusion that the minds of those who suffer from mental illness are biased in ways that make specific thoughts and actions beyond their control.

For those who happen to possess genetic predispositions that diminish specific neurotransmitters like serotonin in their brain, they are likely to act extremely impulsively under certain conditions. Given this neuropsychological predisposition, under the right circumstances, such as economic hardship, this may lead to further problems, such as criminal behavior. Others will have the misfortune of possessing genes that increase the neurochemical reactions that foster a greater likelihood for addiction. For example, a person such as myself, who does not consume alcohol at all because I do not like the taste, must possess a type of brain that, for some reason, allows me to abstain from enjoying and thereby craving the consumption of alcohol. But why is this so? I didn't do anything that would have influenced my desire for abstaining from alcoholic beverages. So what conditions in my life have led me to be biased in this way? What is the difference between my brain and the brain of an alcoholic? How are we biased differently in these respects? An alcoholic's entire life will be negatively affected in varying degrees because of liquids that contain alcohol, whereas my life is entirely unaffected by such beverages. To consider the biological constraints that bias us differently in this regard is to more responsibly understand what factors underlie any person's belief system.

This does not mean that we can never alter or modify our current behavior. There are plenty of programs that deal with addictive behavior. So we have the ability to change or modify our biases when we recognize how they may interfere negatively with our lives. However, the point to note here is that some people will simply be more biologically prone to such biases than others. But even though this may be the case, our lot in life is not completely set in stone. Current research into the neuroplasticity of our brains[3] indicates that the brain has the ability to rewire itself so that the neural signals do not continue to follow pathways that cause human behavior to follow similar patterns. For example, people who suffer from OCD can alter the old ways their brains were accustomed to working. In this way, we can understand how our brains are more *plastic* or flexible.[4] Through specific training techniques, people have been able to overcome PTSD and OCD, and some success has been reported in the treatment of schizophrenia using neural recircuitry techniques.[5] These are but a few of the many ways neuropsychological factors can deeply bias, influence, and affect our beliefs and actions. Understanding better how mental health affects so many of us will go a long way toward better understanding how and why people can be biased in this way and, it is hoped, lead to fairer and more compassionate treatments.

Emotions

It is important to remember that we were emotional beings long before we became so-called rational beings. In other words, when we consider the several million years of cognitive evolution, we become increasingly aware of the fact that the seat of our emotions lies in the midbrain, or limbic system. This area of our brains developed long before the rational, or prefrontal cortex, section of our brains developed. What this translates to is the realization that even the most intelligent among our species can make extremely bad decisions based on their emotions rather than their reason. Just think of how many times intelligent people did bizarre activities that were driven by their emotional investment. One striking example from February 2007 involves love and jealousy between highly intelligent and successful people:

> The police in Orlando, Fla., filed attempted murder charges today against Capt. Lisa Marie Nowak, a NASA astronaut who the authorities say attacked a rival for another astronaut's affection at Orlando International Airport on Monday after driving more than 900 miles from Houston to meet her flight. . . . Captain Nowak, a Navy captain who flew on a shuttle mission last summer, was originally arrested on attempted kidnapping and other charges. . . . When the police arrested Captain Nowak, they found in her possession a steel mallet, a buck knife with a four-inch blade, a BB gun and a map to Captain Shipman's house. . . . According to the police, Captain Nowak drove more than 950 miles from Houston to Orlando to

meet with Captain Shipman, who was flying from Houston to her home in the Orlando area at the same time—because she wanted to confront Captain Shipman after discovering that she too was involved with Commander Oefelein. Captain Nowak, 43, was wearing a trench coat and wig when she was arrested early Monday morning. She told the police she had worn diapers on the journey so that she would not have to stop to use the restroom so she could arrive in time to meet Captain Shipman's flight at the airport.[6]

So what makes a highly intelligent and accomplished astronaut such as Captain Nowak go to such bizarre extremes to demonstrate her love and commitment to another person? Irrationality and poor decision making exists at all levels of intelligence and accomplishment. A PhD or a high-ranking title in no way protects us from our emotions. So-called intelligent people often act irrationally based on pure human emotion, and jealousy is one of the strongest motivating human emotions and one of the most difficult to think critically about—especially when we're the ones affected. This is never the time to scoff or ridicule such people for their behavior. It is a time to sympathize and recognize what difficulties they might have been going through on an emotional and psychological level. None of us are in a position to judge because all of us are prone to emotionally driven passions that occasionally get the better of us.

But what, exactly, are emotions, and why do they have such an overwhelming effect on how we think and behave? Emotions have been defined as affective states—fear, anger, sorrow, joy, disgust, anticipation, surprise, and so on—that can motivate human behavior. There are also more subtle variations, such as terror, phobia, rage, sadness, grief, and happiness. These emotional states are cross-culturally universal. This means that no matter where we travel in the world, we can all recognize when someone is happy, sad, angry, afraid, surprised, and so on. But what causes emotional states, and why do we so often find ourselves at the mercy of them?

As mentioned above, the parts of our brains responsible for our emotional states are located in the center of our brains and are known collectively as the limbic system. The part of our brains responsible for rational decision making is often attributed to the prefrontal cerebral cortex. In terms of cognitive evolution, that is, how and when our brains developed, cognitive scientists believe that the limbic system is much older than the recently developed prefrontal cortex. So it should not be surprising that we often react to information emotionally first and then must think rationally about it afterward. One might even argue that one of the most important skills in critical thinking itself is the ability to recognize one's emotional commitment to some piece of information or a particular situation and then possess the rational maturity to divorce oneself from this commitment while considering it. Easier said than done—but it is a form of disciplined control that becomes easier with practice.

When teaching critical thinking courses, I sometimes demonstrate the power of how emotions can bias our behavior by informing students that I am going to bring out my son's pet tarantula, Harry. I then proceed to tell them that, when he walks out of the holding jar onto the first person's hand, they must very carefully transfer the spider by letting it walk to the next person's hand and so on. I also tell them that my son is very fond of his pet spider, and I do not wish for any damage to come to him. So the students must be very careful in allowing the spider to walk from one of their hands to the next. As I am saying this, I start to observe any students who might be squirming in their seats. This indicates to me that they might be arachnophobes—that they have a great fear (or phobia) of spiders. I then tell them that there is, in fact, no spider but that, in less than a second, their brains had started sending the rest of their bodies messages to flee or to fight. They experienced an increase in adrenaline from specific neuroendocrine influences, which began a process whereby their bodies started to convert sugars to energy. There would also have been an increase in heart and breathing rates. This preparatory time to get ready to respond to the perceived threat all occurs in less than a second. This is just one example of how our own emotional states can bias our behavior. You might be the bravest person on the planet, but when presented with a trigger of a phobia, you would be rendered quite helpless.

Discussing issues that we find emotionally charged often creates an environment in which controlling our biases becomes extremely difficult. If you are passionate about a particular topic—say, in favor of gun control—it may become very difficult to consider what the other side has to say, especially if you have had a personal experience with a particular issue. We will return to this issue in the final chapter of the book. But it is very important for us to look into the mental mirror and consider why we are so passionate about a particular issue. We usually have heated discussions with our friends, relatives, coworkers, colleagues, and so on, so we better figure out how it is we wish to get along. Understanding how our biases influence our thoughts and our actions is one of the clearest ways to help us better understand *why* we have disagreements.

At this point, I want you to take a moment and think about a particular issue on which you have very strong views. It can be about politics, sex, religion, sports, medicine, or *The Bachelor*. Think about the processes that have led you to become so convinced of your view and why you might be less willing or even *un*willing to consider what the other side has to say. This type of bias plays out quite clearly at sporting events. When fans cheer for their team and a player from the other side makes an incredible play, it is often very difficult for the opposing team's fans to acknowledge this feat. I cannot tell you the number of times I have watched mild-mannered friends abandon reason, fairness, and sportsmanship in an effort to win at a particular recreational sport, such as pickup basketball or hockey. And then there are the soccer moms and dads who become over-the-top fanatics when watching their kids play. The very values of athletics, such as fun, sportsmanship, and teamwork, are often eclipsed by the desire to win a competition.

So it is not always easy to keep our biases in check—especially when we have considerable emotional attachment invested in a particular issue. However, with time and practice, it becomes easier. And if this becomes a shared activity where others with whom we disagree practice, it will lead to far more productive discussions about important issues.

Age, Health, and Sex

As we grow older, our values, beliefs, and ideals change. As I have aged, I tend to understand, discuss, believe, and act differently in some ways now than I did as a younger man and certainly as a boy. So age definitely does influence and bias how we perceive and understand information and act on it. This is simply a brute fact of life. The passage from innocence to experience is inevitable. I do not feel differently than I did when I was in my twenties. But I have experienced more at my current age, so I possess a greater capacity to understand and consider and deliberate on issues than I did as a younger man. That's not to say that it's any better or any worse, but age is a factor that biases our understanding of information. Consider the following personal example. When I was about five years old, my mother took me to the family doctor to get a vaccination. It was called a "booster shot," and these follow-up vaccinations were given for measles, whooping cough, and so on to help "boost" one's immune system. However, the way I understood it was that I was getting a "boobster shot." For some reason, I thought both men and women had breasts. I mean, boys and men have nipples. So I just thought there was a process to help speed this along for males. When I got home from the doctor's office, I looked down my T-shirt and asked my mother quite directly, "When do you think I'll get them?" With a rather confused and startled look on her face, my mother quite naturally asked, "Get what?" "My boobs," I said. To this day, I can still picture and hear the thunderous hilarity with which my mother's laughter erupted out of her as family members came running from all corners of the house to determine the cause of her jocularity. She continued to tell this story to family, relatives, and friends for the rest of my life. So age is definitely a factor in biasing how we perceive, interpret, and act on information.

The same could be said for health. As our health changes, our views about issues can be affected or biased because of suffering, pain, or general poor health. Considering important issues just doesn't seem to have the same effect on us when we are busy fighting pain or discomfort due to ill health. This is entirely understandable. Since there is nothing more important to us than our health, it follows that when we are not feeling well, little else matters. So we must be aware of how our health status and the health status of others will bias the manner in which they interpret, consider, and act on information. Just in case you're wondering, the reason that some elderly people are cranky and short-tempered is because they are often in constant pain or discomfort. It's not easy to give a damn when you feel like crap.

As for the differences of sex, much of the literature on sexuality defines us humans on a spectrum from male to female. For the most part, most humans are definitively male or female. But there are transgendered people who defy such strict categorization. Unfortunately, they can face serious identity problems and social backlash due to ignorance and misunderstanding. So I want to be clear and state that I am concentrating my treatment of sexual biases mainly on either end of the spectrum of male or female. Keep in mind that this has nothing to do with social or civil rights. Both sexes and the transgendered have exactly the same rights. What I am referring to instead is the idea that the different biological makeup of males and females has led to distinctions in behaviors that can bias the manner in which information is considered and acted on.

Humans are biologically dimorphic. That means that males tend to be taller, larger, and stronger, with more muscle mass. Females have more estrogen hormone, while males have more testosterone. So far, we cannot see that these are the only factors responsible, but they do tend to point in the direction as to why males tend to be more violent and aggressive than females. To support such a claim, we simply need to look at the world statistics for aggression, crime, murder, and criminal behavior. Men outrank women in this regard by over nine to one.[7] But aside from these biological differences, there have been numerous studies into the physiological, hormonal, and neuronal differences between males and females that have provided important information in the treatment of gender-specific diseases, the function of medications, different procedures for surgeries, and so on. Although males and females differ genetically only by a single Y chromosome, both sexes differ considerably in specific biological ways. So we must realize that these differences will bias the way in which both sexes interpret, revise, retain, and act on information.

In terms of mental health, recent studies now indicate that men and women suffering from schizophrenia respond differently to odors and scents. Such a finding can help better treat those suffering from such a neurodegenerative disease. University of Dayton psychologist Julie Walsh-Messinger found that scents are important because neurodegenerative diseases like schizophrenia are known to affect the sense of smell. Odor has a direct line to the brain's emotional processing. As Walsh-Messinger explains, "The neural structures that process smell and emotion are closely related, so understanding how they interact might help us better understand the emotional and social impairments associated with schizophrenia." Walsh-Messinger's study, published in the journal *Psychiatry Research*, asked twenty-six people with schizophrenia and twenty-seven without to rate odors for their pleasantness and unpleasantness. There were no differences between men and women without schizophrenia. However, when Walsh-Messinger looked at men and women with schizophrenia who had increased symptoms of depression, the women rated neutral odors more unpleasant, and the men rated them more pleasant. Men with schizophrenia and women without the disorder also judged pleasant odors as more unpleasant than did men without the disorder.[8] Walsh-Messinger is now conducting further studies in the hopes of determining the cause of these differences in men and women.

These represent just a few of the examples of how we can better understand the ways in which biological factors bias us as a species.

CULTURAL BIASES

It is important to note that, just as biological factors have considerable influence over what we believe and how we act, culture plays just as important a role. There are hundreds of developed cultures throughout the world, so it should come as little surprise that social norms and cultural biases will influence the way we see, understand, and interact with the world. Here are just a few of the main types of cultural biases.

Family Upbringing

When you were growing up, how were you raised and by whom? Did you come from a home with a mother and father? A single-parent home? One with two dads or two moms? Were you raised by your siblings, relatives, or grandparents? Or were you raised by pigeons in the wilds of Central Park? Our family life plays a huge and important role in how we see and understand the world. How strict or lax your caregivers or parents were with regard to your behavior will have a profound impact on you. Some of us were given a curfew to be home at a certain time. Others were not. Was it a family rule that you had to eat everything on your plate before leaving the table? Did you have to do chores around the house? Take out the trash? Do the dishes? Rake the leaves? Were you allowed to date any person you liked? If you are gay or transgender, how was this dealt with in your home?

Families develop entire lifestyles and habits around how things get done in a day. Who takes out the trash, cuts the lawn, does the dishes, or looks after the shopping and what television programs and Internet sites are suitable for viewing—these are all aspects of home life that influence or bias your behavior later in life. Violating such rules of the family household can and often does lead to challenges. Consider your behavior right now and think for a moment on how much of your day-to-day life is regulated by family patterns of behavior developed from the time you were born.

Ethnicity

The topic of immigration seems to be a constant concern in the United States and elsewhere throughout the world. People within one country become angry over the number of so-called foreigners invading and taking jobs away from its citizens. This type of fear or hatred—or *xenophobia*—is a complex issue, but it often centers on differences in ethnicity. How we have come to define ourselves ethnically often plays a crucial role in how we understand issues. The values, customs, habits, and rituals of our various ethnicities can present barriers of understanding and incite dislike for others simply because they do not belong to the same group. This is known as *nationalistic tribalism*. There are several theories as to why humans do this, but for the most part, it harkens back to evolutionary times when we lived in small groups, were largely nomadic, and subsisted on whatever we could find, scavenge, hunt, or discover. If our ancestors came in contact with other nomadic groups, their options would have been limited: fight, flee, or befriend. During a time without police, lawyers, judges, courts, and prisons, life and survival would truly have been red in tooth and claw. There would have been no advanced knowledge of the manner or degree to which tribes would have cohabitated. Some encounters would have been peaceful. Others would have ended with a violent massacre, rape, and pillaging. The saying "Better safe than sorry" comes to mind as a central doctrine for such times. This evolutionary baggage of xenophobia is still with us today. It is also present in all other animals as well—and for good reason. For our human ancestors, being wary of potential threats to life and limb rather than suffer the slings and arrows of outrageous marauders is just good advice to live by during such dangerous times. So we, like every other animal, are naturally xenophobic—that is, fearful of that or those who are foreign to us. This, however, does not mean we must stay this way permanently. In fact, once we determine a lack of threat to us, we can welcome those who seem unlikely to harm us. This is why you can feed pigeons and squirrels who sit on your knees on park benches in city parks: they have learned that people with food are no longer a threat. Now, for the most part, we tolerate and even celebrate the ethnic differences we find in our multicultural communities. But we still find that the beliefs, rituals, and actions of one ethnic group often clash with those of another. We have seen this type of ethnic hatred carried out in much more horrific forms today with warring in Syria, Congo, Yemen, Darfur, India and Pakistan, and so on, and we are seeing signs of nationalism occurring around the globe, including the United States. So before you can become a better thinker, you need to consider to what extent your ethnic values and attachment to ethnic ways of life influence the ways in which you see the world and consider any issue.

Religion

In terms of the distribution of those of religious belief across our planet, Pew Research (2018) lists the percentages of world religions as follows:[9]

Christians: 31.2 percent (2.3 billion)
Muslims: 24.1 percent (1.8 billion)
Unaffiliated: 16 percent (1.2 billion)
Hindus: 15.1 percent (1.1 billion)
Buddhists: 6.9 percent (550 million)
Folk religions: 5.7 percent (400 million)
Other religions: 0.8 percent (100 million)
Jews: 0.2 percent (14.4 million)

This means that about 84 percent of people on this planet maintain beliefs in some supernatural elements of reality, such as Gods, angels, saints, and various other aspects of divination.

It should come as no surprise that religion has—and continues to have—a considerable influence over human behavior. If you consider yourself a religious person, take some time to consider how you came to develop your current metaphysical beliefs. The most common path of religious indoctrination comes to us from our parents. It is impossible for infants, toddlers, and young children to rationally think about

Figure 2.1.   World Religions

religious doctrine that is taught to them by their parents and practiced and celebrated throughout their communities. It is not until a person reaches a certain age of maturity that they begin to question their religious beliefs. For those who were not indoctrinated into a specific faith, there are many cases in which, as adults, many gravitate toward a particular religion for specific reasons or needs. By far, one of the greatest appeals to religious practice is the communal sense of support that can be found when like-minded individuals gather for a common purpose. There is no lack of evidence indicating the neural rewards that come not only with religious conviction but also in celebrating that conviction within a community, and there is little doubt that religiously motivated people have done wonderful and amazing things for humanity. Although many atrocities have been committed in the name of various gods and religions, religious faith has also contributed to some spectacular examples of love, compassion, art, and devotion. Regardless of the effects of religious belief and influence, there is little denying that it has biased and continues to bias billions of people on this planet.

Religious belief provides people with outlooks on life that greatly influence how they think and act—both positively and negatively. But there are times when dissonance and disagreement arise due to conflicts between faith and science. For example, many devout or orthodox world religions do not accept homosexuality as a fact of biology but instead see it as a life choice that violates their god's wishes. To be a homosexual, then, is to act in ways that are in direct opposition to how a particular god wants us to behave. So if a devout person of faith happens to have a close relation—such as a son or a daughter—who happens to be gay, it may be difficult to reconcile their love of their child with the will, teachings, or commandments of their god. And this is not an easy reconciliation. In fact, many students have told me that their parents have stopped speaking to them after they have come out as gay due to their family's religious beliefs. I am not deliberately attempting to denigrate or bash religious belief here but simply trying to demonstrate how powerful this bias can be when considering information. We will return to this topic in the final chapter of the book.

Geographic Location

Of all the places you could have been born in this world, why did it turn out to be where your parents resided at that time? Consider now in which part of the world you were raised. If you have always lived in a developed part of the world, how do you think your views of the world, yourself, and others might differ if you were raised in a developing nation thousands of miles from where you now live? The very fact that you live in a particular part of the world will have a profound influence on how you interpret and act on information. How people in Switzerland will understand one nation's foreign policies will be vastly different from those who live in Middle Eastern countries. But geographic location can be even more specific than this. For example, consider the identities and differences between provinces in Canada, states in the United

States, and regions of England, India, Australia, Mexico, and so on. Rivalries often develop between neighboring cities, like the fictional rivalry between Springfield and Shelbyville in *The Simpsons* or the sometimes violent confrontations that exist between football fans—both in soccer and in American football.

The sense of regional community that can develop in a given part of the world can become thoroughly ingrained in our lives. This instills within us a comparative ability to view differing customs, actions, and attitudes in a way that might make us think, "That's not how we do things around here." So even our regional geography can bias us according to our preferred in-group ways of doing things. Therefore, we must develop the intellectual maturity to understand that we could have just as easily become a New York Yankees fan rather than a Los Angeles Dodgers fan if our parents had lived on the eastern side of New York State rather than in California.

Education

The way in which people are educated directly biases the manner in which they perceive, interpret, understand, and act on information. We can define education in a very broad sense, ranging from information learned within the home to more formal settings, such as primary, middle, secondary, and postsecondary institutions. Just think about how differently students are taught in urban classrooms in the United States compared to that of an all-boys Taliban school in rural Pakistan. In Canada, Great Britain, and the United States, all children have access to school systems, which generally teach boys and girls equally. The Taliban, however, teach boys only, and the main learning text is the Koran. For mathematical skills, boys have been asked to count with AK-47s and to subtract by killing off members of rival groups. So where and how you were educated will contribute greatly to how you interpret, revise, retain, and act on information.

Education applies to everyday practical activities, ranging from dating to grocery shopping to buying a house. Consider automobile driving. Some young drivers will have taken driving lessons (for those who can afford them). Others will not. People develop driving habits based on geographic driving styles and constraints. For someone raised in North America, driving in the United Kingdom can be quite a

Figure 2.2.   Education

challenge. There, drivers sit on the right side of the vehicle but drive on the left side of the road, but in North America, it's just the opposite. In addition, most cars in the United Kingdom and Europe are standard, or manual, requiring the use of a clutch and a stick shift, whereas in North America, most cars are automatic. No matter where we learned to drive, however, there are some basic universal "rules of the road" that apply to all drivers no matter where they happen to be driving. One of those universal rules for traveling on highways is to avoid tailgating, or driving extremely close behind the driver in front of you, especially at high speeds. Part of my work as an educator and consultant is to provide psychological counseling. Most of my clients are motor vehicle accident victims. Over the years, it has become increasingly apparent that those who have experienced car accidents will often suffer from PTSD to the point that driving again is very troublesome. Many accident victims report considerable anxiety when faced with circumstances similar to their recent accident, and many of those victims suffered from rear-end collisions because drivers were following too closely behind them. Let's face it: what, if any, is the practical purpose of tailgating? Can a decent, sound argument be put forward for tailgating on a high-speed highway? Not really. Many of us will have experienced drivers who tailgate. There is a very basic correlation that the faster one is driving, the less room is left as a margin of error. Therefore, should the person being tailgated step on their brakes suddenly, the tailgater has very little time to respond, and the result is most often a rear-end collision. It is a very dangerous driving technique, one that causes considerable stress not only for the one being tailgated but also for everyone in the vicinity of the tailgater. In fact, the entire environment around the tailgater becomes highly stressful. So an important takeaway lesson that I have learned is that we should always be aware of other drivers and what their particular psychological biases might be. We have no idea who is in those other cars and what psychological trauma they may currently be facing. We would do well to include in the education of young drivers a section devoted to understanding psychological bias.

We must never lose sight of the fact that one of the central purposes of education is to open the minds of those seeking knowledge and to impart in them important, interesting, and helpful information along with sound critical thinking skills. But education can also be used to indoctrinate specific beliefs, thereby stifling free and critical thinking along with introspection and the thirst for knowledge. Take a moment to think about how you were educated in all aspects of life and the ways in which this has influenced you in your abilities to think critically. How differently might you now see the world had you been educated differently in another country or even region of the world? How might your future education—including this book—change the way in which you will consider and act on information?

Friends

Throughout our lives, we come into close contact with various people with whom we seek out, develop, and value their companionship and friendship. The influence our friends have on us is undeniable. From the time of our youth, we have been actively involved in making friends and becoming associated with an intricate connection of influences. Take a moment to think back about that most awkward developmental stage in life: adolescence. With our brains awash in a bath of hormonal soup and our bodies adjusting to bigger and different parts, we began to see ourselves developing independently from parental guidance and control. Individual as well as peer and group pressures have contributed to how we view ideas and issues, and sometimes conformity is much easier to accept than independence. Since it is virtually impossible for any of us to live in total isolation, unaffected by others, the friendships we make leave lasting impressions on us. Something to keep in mind at this point is how influential *you* are on your network of friends and how influential *they* are on you. To what degree do you or can you have meaningful discussions with your friends? Do you always tend to agree? We saw earlier how easy it is to agree. How do you and your friends deal with disagreement? Can you accept that you will have differences of opinions? Having important discussions and disagreeing is often a test for friendship, and how well a friendship survives such disagreements often solidifies and strengthens or damages and tears apart friendships.

So it is often the case that even complete strangers will simply conform to dissonant ideas to preserve the perceived status quo. There is a classic example that demonstrates how easy it is for people to conform. In a prank television show from the 1960s and 1970s called *Candid Camera*, three people get into an elevator in which there is a single gentleman in a trench coat holding the doors open for them. When all three people get in the elevator, they face the wall of the elevator rather than the doors. In a short while, the man in the trench coat joins them and turns around and faces the wall. There have been other psychological experiments demonstrating conformity to group opinion and behavior. During the 1950s, Professor Solomon Asch conducted a series of conformity experiments at Swarthmore College that continue to influence conformity experiments today. In one of his experiments, a group of men look at three lines on a piece of paper, all of which have different lengths. They are then asked to determine if a separate line matches the lengths of either of the other three. All the males are secretly a part of the study with only one male unknowingly being the test subject. The first two or three examples are easy to determine, and all agree which line is the match. However, on the fourth try, the line is clearly shorter than the one to which all men agree. In most of the trials, the test subject ends up agreeing with the rest of the men even though he knows it is clearly wrong.

Another striking contemporary experiment demonstrating conformity involves a group of actors and one subject sitting in a room in which a fire is staged. Smoke begins to pour into the room from beneath a doorway, and a smoke alarm goes off, yet none of the people leave the room. The test subject often appears nervous and agitated but, more often than not, does not leave the room or investigate the source of the fire. Even when there is a perceived threat to a person's health, this can be overridden by peer pressure and group conformity. Such experiments make obvious the need for us to be aware of the extent to which such external influences can bias our thinking and our behavior.

Media

Today, we have incredibly fast access to more information than at any time in history. We are constantly inundated with information coming from various forms of media, such as the Internet, television, movies, music, newspapers, magazines, and art. But as we saw in this book's introduction, there has been an increasing rise in what is known as fake news (especially online). This involves information that can appear on Twitter or Facebook or other such sites in which people have deliberately created fake or false information to appear as though it is reliable. As we saw in chapter 1, *reliability* is one of the universal foundational criteria on which our premises must rest in order for an argument to be considered solid. So we must always be on our guard against such fake accounts of information and possess the media literacy skills that allow us to make discernments between reliable and fake information. We have to empower ourselves with the critical thinking skills that will allow us to recognize when information is not factual. If we are not mentally vigilant in this regard, then we are suckers and will believe anything we see, read, or are told. This is the very antithesis of being a good critical thinker. We must show due diligence in our quest to confirm or falsify information and ensure that it has been attained in a reliable manner. Otherwise, we subject ourselves to uncorroborated fake news that can spread faster than we are capable of stopping; as Mark Twain so aptly put, "A lie can travel half way around the world while the truth is putting on its shoes."[10] So we cannot simply believe everything we see or read just because it's on the Internet, in a magazine, or on television.

To be a good critical thinker, you must constantly question the source of your information. Do you get it mostly from online sources? Television? Newspapers? Magazines? The school yard? Your neighbor? Be aware that all information—no matter which type—comes to you already biased (including this very book). There is no such thing as bias-neutral information. Whether you watch *Fox and Friends* or *The Daily Show* or turn on CNN News, MSNBC, or Al Jazeera, the information you receive will have a particular bias or political slant to it. Recognizing the political ideologies behind the media you receive will empower you with the ability to acknowledge how a particular source wants you to interpret the information. Never forget that everyone has an agenda—from your local librarian to the president of the United States. It is sometimes difficult for humans to play fairly and get along, especially when it comes to discussing important issues, because our agendas and our biases often get in the way and limit us in this regard.

Bias Check: Biases Are Filters of Information

By now, it should be apparent that everything you think and everything you do is the result of your biological and cultural biases. You now need to do a *bias check* and become aware that any new information presented to you must pass through a series of biased filters before you can accept it, reject it, or remain neutral to it.

It is a part of our nature to favor information that confirms our own biases. This is perfectly normal. In many respects, this is what it means to be human. However, in critical thinking, we develop the ability to acknowledge what our biases are in an effort to more fairly understand why it is we believe what we do and why it is we act according to those particular beliefs. In this way, we become more critically reflective of our beliefs, ideas, and opinions and thus more humble in our assertions and fairer in our treatment of others whose beliefs, ideas, and opinions may differ from our own. As with news services, it is often difficult to diminish our own biases and vested interests in order to objectively consider and act on the *facts*. For example, just think of the 2018 Senate hearing to determine whether Brett Kavanaugh should have been appointed as an associate justice of the Supreme Court. On which side did you come down? Did you think Dr. Blasey Ford's testimony was compelling enough to convince you that Kavanaugh should not be appointed? Or did you think that she was either lying or misguided in her testimony and that she was being used as a pawn by the Democrats to smear Kavanaugh's name and stall the procedure of appointing a Republican to the highest legal position in the land? Or did you think along completely different lines? Or were you simply

Figure 2.3.   Bias Filters

neutral to the entire proceeding? Whatever you now believe is the direct result of years of influences that have biased you in ways that often unconsciously influence you to seek out information that confirms your current entrenched biases. Information that runs counter to what you currently believe is often discounted, ignored, or otherwise forgotten because it creates dissonance within us. This feeling of unease creates discord and tension, so it is perfectly natural and human to want to avoid it.[11] However, we must grow up intellectually if we are to be responsible, critical thinkers. This means that we must honestly, even courageously, look at ourselves and our biases so that we can recognize when they are standing in the way of fairness and clarity of thought because this is what we would want others to do for us. Never forget that *fairness* will always be the Golden Rule of critical thinking.

So we must learn to recognize cultural biases, both in others and in ourselves, because these often distort sound reasoning, leading to unwarranted and poorly supported conclusions. It is difficult to acknowledge our own biases, especially when we are emotionally connected to a particular issue. But in order to argue clearly and present our ideas in a precise, consistent, and fair manner, we must learn to recognize and compensate for our biases. This is not easy. That is why critical thinking takes time, effort, and repetition, and it is why the most difficult part of becoming a good critical thinker is to acknowledge any biases in yourself that may distort your reasoning.

Personal Bias Profile

At this point, it would be a good idea to take some time to do a bias check and consider what biases have influenced you the most at this point in your life. Ask yourself what you think when you consider important issues like abortion, euthanasia, gun control, religion, sex, and so on. Take a moment to write down what you perceive to be your most influential biases.

Biological Biases
1. Genetic
2. Neuropsychological
3. Emotional
4. Age, sex, and health

Social Biases
1. Ethnicity
2. Family
3. Religion
4. Geography
5. Education
6. Friends
7. Media

After completing this list, you should begin to see a *personal bias profile* develop. The purpose of the profile is to develop an honest and more complete understanding of yourself that will provide insight into how and why you now think the way you do. Once you have completed your personal bias profile, you will be in a better position to understand why it is you believe and act the way you do. In so doing, you will be better equipped to recognize how biases influence belief and action— not only in yourself but in others as well. There was a *Seinfeld* episode that aired on November 4, 1993, in which the female lead character, Elaine, starts dating a gentleman, Lloyd Braun, who works as an adviser to the mayor of New York City, David Dinkins, who is running against Rudy Giuliani. Elaine suggests to Lloyd that everyone living in New York should wear name tags so that it would make everyone feel more familiar and friendly toward one another. Of course, when Lloyd suggests the idea to Dinkins, the idea is publicly ridiculed, and Lloyd gets fired as a result. But perhaps Elaine didn't go far enough. What if everyone had to wear tags that indicated their personal bias profiles? Would this lead to greater transparency and honesty in personal and professional relationships? Or might it make things worse? We will probably never know.

CONFIRMATION BIAS, FAIRNESS, AND GETTING ALONG

So we have arrived at the most difficult part of learning how to think: acknowledging our biases, playing fairly, and getting along.

Everyone likes to be right—or, at least, everyone likes the *feeling* of being right. This feeling of being right provides us with a neurochemical reward, accompanied by a sense of control, empowerment, security, and status. As we grow and mature, so too do our beliefs become entrenched through various biological and cultural biases. It is perfectly normal, then, that we all fall victim to *confirmation bias*. Take a moment to consider your current beliefs regarding, say, gun control (another topic we consider in the final chapter). Why do you believe what you do in relation to this topic? In what context did you develop your views? What evidence do you rely on to support your views? Whether you believe all guns should be destroyed or everyone should be able to carry loaded weapons anywhere they travel, your entrenched views developed over time. Whether you are aware of this or not, we tend to look more favorably toward information and evidence that support our views and to ignore information and evidence that disconfirm or fail to support them. This type of positive feedback loop of support feeds and confirms our already established biases about issues. Perhaps a definition of confirmation bias is best summed up in a paraphrase of Paul Simon's lyrics from the song "The Boxer": a person hears what they want to hear and disregards the rest. So, we can never escape our biases. But at least we can acknowledge them and do our best to make sure that they have not clouded our abilities to think critically about important issues.

The ancient Egyptians and Greeks had a wonderful model for humankind's struggle with their biases. They used the analogy of a chariot rider to represent reason and a horse as human passion or emotion. In learning *how* to think, we must imagine that the horse we must try to control is our biases. We must steer the horse down a path of facts and evidence toward the truth—however difficult this may be. We must become better angels of our nature in this regard and resist the lure of allowing our biases to get the better of us. For, if they do get the better of us, then all value in truth, accuracy, reliability, and even common sense is lost, and the cost of losing is simply too high.

As we saw earlier, fairness acts as the Golden Rule of dialogue. In other words, we must abide by the rules of fairness when considering the ideas and biases of others, just as we would want others to do for us. Playing fairly and getting along are some of the first rules instilled in kids when they are sent off to play with other children. Yet they are rules that we all too soon abandon as we age. The reason for this is that much that happens in the world is perceived by many to be unfair. We are often led to believe that there is precious little justice in life. We are often victims of unfairness—sometimes to the point of cruelty, despair, and ruin. So for me to say that we must "play fairly" may sound like a piece of advice you would just as soon skip over. But I must tell you that, as an ideal, fairness always wins out over deception and cheating. Fairness is also the cornerstone of critical thinking. If everyone plays by the rules of critical thinking and abides by the Golden Rule of dialogue, everyone will get more of what they want. But this requires cooperation and understanding.

Let's face it: sometimes it's not easy to be fair. We all like to win. We all have egos, goals for status and resources, ambitions, biases, and the drive to succeed (some more than others). So it should come as no surprise that we like to be right when it comes to making a point or taking a position. When confronted with an opposing view, one of the most difficult things to do in critical thinking is to accept it as a good argument (even if you disagree with it). To use a sports analogy, this is not unlike acknowledging a great goal scored against your team. Good educators should be able to read student assignments without having their personal, political, or philosophical biases affect grades. Likewise, good bosses should acknowledge when an employee makes a good point counter to his or her own. In addition, good politicians should admit their biases (and mistakes) and acknowledge good ideas from opposing party members. Yes, these are intellectual ideals, but they are important ideals that are easy to forget. We are not all going to agree all of the time. Disagreements are a fact of life. But by understanding how our biases and those of others influence the ways in which we interpret, understand, and act on information, we can better appreciate why differences of opinion exist and why disagreements develop. In so doing, we can go a long way toward understanding the uniqueness of individual thought. This will allow us to more amicably and fairly resolve differences, mediate disagreements, and initiate dialogue that is productive and respectful to both sides regardless of the outcome.

Be aware of biases. Know yours and those of others. In so doing, we will be better prepared to understand differences of opinions, beliefs, and actions. You now know the importance of argumentation, reasoning, and biases. These are important tools to master in the skill set of critical thinking, which will teach you *how* to think about important issues. Now that we know what arguments are and how biases contribute to the ways in which we interpret, understand, revise, and act on information, we can turn our attention to the next tool in learning how to think: *context*. As we shall see, understanding the context in which information arises is often just as important as the information itself.

• 3 •

Context Is Key

*W*hen we are discussing the critical thinking tool of context, what we are really talking about are things like time, place, and circumstance. Context allows us to better understand the framework and the backstory behind information. Understanding context allows a critical thinker a broader understanding of the way in which information is housed and its connection to emotions, vested interests, and incentives. It is within the aspect of context that we also find the importance of *fact checking*. If we fail to properly identify the relevant facts behind information, if we fail in checking on the backstory behind information, or if we come up lacking in identifying the who, what, why, where, when, and how behind information, then our opinions regarding that information may very well be misguided and our likelihood of fairly assessing it considerably decreased. For example, when there was a string of deadly assaults against individual black men in the United States starting in 2013 with the acquittal of Trayvon Martin's murderer, George Zimmerman, there was a reaction from the African American community—in particular, Alicia Garza, Patrisse Cullors, and Opal Tometi, who created a black-centered political movement called #BlackLivesMatter.[1] Over time, various people in white communities in the country began to co-opt the name of this movement and came out with the statement "All Lives Matter." Although we can agree that all lives do, in fact, matter, what is missing from this declaration is the context that gave rise to the movement that generated the original "Black Lives Matter" slogan and hashtag. We must remember that it was the contextual incentive of racially motivated injustice that brought about the origin of the statement and movement behind #Black Lives Matter, which then brought considerable attention to the inequities of policing against young urban black men.

It is important to be able to identify context in relation to arguments or information because if we fail to do this adequately, we may form opinions too quickly and therefore react unfairly in the assessment of that information. This can generate what is known as a *straw man fallacy*. We discuss this fallacy and several others in greater detail in chapter 6. For now, it is important to understand why such a fallacy exists as an error in reasoning related to the importance of context. A straw man argument is a metaphor that refers to the creation or fabrication of information that was not what a person intended. In other words, if one misinterprets information either deliberately or unconsciously and then proceeds to comment or criticize that wrong interpretation, everything the person states has no *relevance*. As we saw in chapter 1, if an argument is to be accepted, the premises must satisfy universal criteria—one of which is relevance. When anyone misinterprets information and presents it as the intended argument, they have created an artificial, or straw man, version of a person's argument, therefore rendering any criticism they have to say about it as misguided and ineffective. In case you're wondering why it's called a straw man argument, the term is a metaphor that references the way in which nineteenth-century soldiers in a militia would practice bayonet combat activities on fake soldiers made out of straw. So, the infantrymen were not attacking real soldiers but straw soldiers. In the same way, if we either deliberately or unconsciously misrepresent another person's argument and then proceed to critique the misrepresentation, this is metaphorically similar to attacking a straw man. The straw man fallacy is a fallacy of relevance because any critique lobbied against the misrepresentation is irrelevant. Because fairness is the cornerstone of critical thinking, we must practice due diligence in accurately representing another person's beliefs, ideas, and arguments. Today, this is called *steelmanning*. Instead of unconsciously or deliberately misrepresenting another person's views, steelmanning is the attempt to understand and express an opposing person's argument in its best possible light—even to the point of improving it, if possible. This demonstrates intellectual maturity as well as civil consideration, which are expected on both sides of a discussion. So, instead of simply contradicting another person's beliefs, the method of steelmanning allows us to genuinely express interest and consideration for their views even though we may disagree with them.

It is important to understand that in any culture, all language is embroiled within a context in which people try to say not only what they are thinking but also how they are biased, and the setting in which these interactions are taking place often provides the context underlying the information. When we properly understand context, we are in a better position to understand the reasons that people might think and act in particular ways that might differ from their own. Psychology professor Daniel Willingham from the University of Virginia maintains that context, or what he calls "content knowledge," is extremely important in understanding another's argument, ideas, beliefs, and so on. Willingham states, "In some circumstances, even toddlers can understand principles of conditional reasoning and in other circumstances, conditional reasoning confuses adults physicians . . . it all depends on the content of the problem."[2] There are many examples of the importance of context. There was an old episode of *Star Trek* from the 1960s in which the science officer, Mr. Spock, tries to commandeer USS *Enterprise* off its original course and on a direct route to Spock's home planet, Vulcan.[3] Nobody knows why Spock is acting all out of sorts as it were, that is, until we find out that Spock must return to his home planet within eight days in order to take part in a ritual known as Pon Farr—a mating ritual—or he will die. So like a salmon swimming upstream to go fertilize eggs and then potentially die in the attempt, poor Spock, with his pointed ears and blue shirt (and bluer balls), must literally make his trek across the stars of the galaxy in search of a mate. Once we, the viewers, understand why Spock needs to return to his home planet, we are in a better position to understand the motive behind his erratic behavior. Without this context, we might judge Spock too harshly and unfairly.

The same would be true regarding the way in which people in one country try to understand what's going on in another country. For people living outside the region of a specific country, it might be difficult to grasp or appreciate the nuances that form the context within which a given event is occurring. For example, what is going on now in 2020 in Yemen is a major travesty. Yet in Canada, Europe, Asia, or the United States, we hardly hear anything about the atrocities that are taking place by Saudi Arabia against the people of Yemen. If we wanted to learn more about what is happening in Yemen at this point in time, we would need to ask ourselves what resources would be available for us to access in order to make more reasoned opinions based on more solid arguments further supported by evidence about what is actually happening there.[4] This, of course, brings up the issue of fact checking.

"JUST THE FACTS, PLEASE"

For the record, a *fact* is most often defined as a thing or information or a statement that has been demonstrated to be true often by appeals to evidence. *Opinion*, on the other hand, is a personal judgment about some thing or information or statement that is not necessarily based on fact, knowledge, proof, or certainty. The *New York Times* has issued guidelines and online courses to assist in training people to better understand information and to make discernments between what can be considered factual and what is simply opinion. You can even take a quiz to test how well you are capable of this critical thinking skill.[5] A major study, titled "Distinguishing between Factual and Opinion Statements in the News," found that "the politically aware, digitally savvy and those more trusting of the news media fare better; Republicans and Democrats both influenced by political appeal of statements."[6] There are various other online resources that one might find useful to fact-check or further research information regarding a particular issue: *Snopes, Pressbook: Web Literacy, Politifact, Factcheck.org, Washington Post Fact Checker, Truth Be Told, NPR Fact-Check, Lie Detector* (Univision, Spanish language), *Hoax Slayer, Climate Feedback, SciCheck, Quote Investigator, FactsCan* (Canada), *TrudeauMetre* (Canada), *El Polígrafo* (Mexico), *The Hound* (Mexico), *Guardian Reality Check* (United Kingdom), *BBC Reality Check* (United Kingdom), *Full Fact* (United Kingdom), *mediabiasfactcheck.com, civilination.org, domainbigdata.com,* and *newswise.ca.*[7] This list is not meant to be exhaustive of the resources available; rather, it illustrates some of the helpful and trusted sites that one may access when determining the reliability and truthfulness of information.

So when we try to understand what is going on in other parts of the world, we must also appreciate and accept that our privileged view often has a limited contextual background. Since I am removed from other worlds and I must, by nature and by culture, experience that information through various filtered and biased views belonging not only to myself but also to those of any given news editors, I may never be getting the complete story and may find myself separated from some of the most important contextual information regarding the particular issue that is taking place.

So, then, to what extent can we trust the information we receive through various forms of media? This leads us to consider a second foundational criterion in our efforts to appreciate the context of information: *reliability*. If the information presented to us has not been established in a reliable manner, we may not be able to appropriately comment on the actual intent or factual nature of the information. As we saw during the 2016 U.S. presidential election, there was a great deal of fake news circulating online not only from Facebook and Twitter but from dozens of other sites as well. If we use any of the information from such fake sources as premises for our conclusions, we have failed to appreciate the context in which that information was presented and therefore have failed to satisfy the foundational criterion of reliability. In this manner, we would not be treating the information or those to whom the information applies fairly because such information has come from unreliable sources. Remember that we can't just believe anything we want simply because it *feels* true. Truth and facts are not subject to feelings. The world does not care if you feel that Bigfoot exists. The facts of the matter state otherwise. Show me some facts, such as a body of a Sasquatch—either living or dead—and I must follow where the evidence leads.

Not only must we consider how *relevant* and *reliable* our sources of information are regarding context, but we are also led to consider the universal foundational criterion of *sufficiency*: in other words, when is enough background information, time, and circumstance *sufficient* to provide the context required for us to make a fair interpretation of information?

It is important to appreciate context, and in so doing, we need to be careful how we interpret information about any important issue. We have to take the time to make sure that we have a sufficient amount of background information so that we can fully appreciate the context in which that information has been presented. The criterion of sufficiency applies to determining the extent to which we have fulfilled our obligation in determining the context of information. It is always difficult to know exactly when we have established a sufficient context. Just as it is difficult to know when we have established a sufficient number of

Figure 3.1. Where is Bigfoot?

premises to support a conclusion, so too is it difficult to know when we have sufficiently satisfied understanding the context of a given issue. There are no hard-and-fast rules in determining this. New information can always be added to bring further contextual grounding to a particular issue. So we are, by nature, always open-ended in how we accept the conclusions of arguments, for new information may come to light or the context may take on a different hue or nuance, adding to the information and thereby affecting the overall determination of its sufficiency.

For example, context sometimes plays an important role in discussing the subject of abortion. There are generally three schools of thought when it comes to discussing this issue. First there are conservatives. Conservatives believe that life and rights should be granted to an organism as soon as sperm touches egg. Once this occurs, a conservative maintains that no interference can come between the now developing zygote and fetus and its eventual anticipated birth. At the other end of the spectrum are the legalists. This is also a feminist perspective. The legalist–feminist perspective maintains that a developing human organism is deserving of rights both legal and moral once the head and shoulders have exited the birth canal. Prior to that point, the mother is in complete control over what happens to the developing fetus; her rights are paramount and supersede those of the fetus up and until its head and shoulders have exited the birth canal. Finally, the third position on abortion is known as the gradualist position. The gradualist maintains that life and therefore human rights—both moral and legal—occur somewhere between conception and birth. In other words, the developing fetus literally becomes "more alive" as it develops within the womb. Therefore, the gradualist believes that a developing fetus is more alive at nine months than it is at two weeks.

So how does context play into the controversial issue of abortion? Let's imagine that a person is very much pro-life and that she believes that life begins at conception and is therefore defined as a conservative. Such a person would believe that humans should not interfere with the developing maturation of the fetus. However, how would any conservative feel if they knew that the context of the pregnancy was the result of the incestuous rape by a father of his thirteen-year-old daughter? Or we could maneuver the variables in any way we wanted in order to make the outcome of the developing fetus the result of very undesirable or heinous actions. We could say that the developing fetus has no brain whatsoever. In this case, an anencephalic fetus will not survive much longer than a few seconds after birth—should it make it to the third trimester. Given this context, the gradualist might state that it is more humane to abort this particular fetus as early on in its developmental stage as possible. In this way, we could avoid further development of the nervous system and the potential for the fetus to experience pain. A conservative might still disagree, but at least we can consider scenarios with changing contexts that might push the limits of a particular school of thought.

At the other end of the spectrum, we can challenge the legalist by imagining a scenario in which a woman was one contraction away from giving birth. According to the legalist, the fetus's head and shoulders have not yet exited the birth canal. Therefore, it follows that, if so desired, the delivering mother still has the option to end the life of the very-soon-to-be-born infant. If it is difficult for a legalist to agree with this request since the infant will literally be born in a few seconds, do they need to reconsider the entailments of their belief about human rights? The point I am trying to make clear here is whether context could change the beliefs of various perspectives regarding the issue of abortion. In other words, are there any contextual situations in which our beliefs might change or become revised? This is why when we discuss important issues like abortion, we really need to use philosophical thought experiments to imagine scenarios that might challenge our currently held views to see how far we are willing to stand by our opinions and beliefs. In this way, we can test our resolve, and in so doing, we can become more mature in the development of our ideas. In addition, such challenges allow us to have civil disagreements and become able to reflectively and proactively challenge one another's beliefs and opinions. This is how we evolve, develop, and mature intellectually not only as individuals but also as nations and especially as an entire world population. Without this type of civility, we are reduced to shouting past one another, which produces very little insight and wastes enormous amounts of time, energy, and money.

"THAT WAS TAKEN OUT OF CONTEXT!"

In remembering the importance of context to critical thinking, consider how many times you might have read or heard someone say the phrase "That was taken out of context!" What this refers to is an unfair interpretation of information regarding a particular issue that is often due to a misunderstanding of the surroundings and circumstances in which the information was situated. It is also sometimes the result of a simple lack of factual information. In other words, sometimes we just don't have enough facts to formulate an opinion, belief, or position. There is an interesting example that became a television and Internet viral meme involving a story about an incident at a Chicago Cubs baseball game.[8] In one scene, a foul ball was hit down the third base line and one of the ball boys catches and then throws the ball to a small child sitting in the bleachers just a short distance away. The child fumbles the ball, which falls between his seat and rolls to the second row, where a man reaches down, picks it up, and hands it to his wife instead of back to the child. At first glance, it would seem that the man was acting senselessly and selfishly. However, context—in the form of a backstory—revealed that the man seated in the second row had already given that particular child a baseball earlier as well as another baseball to another child nearby. His wife jokingly stated that she hadn't received a ball yet. After he gave her the ball, she then gave it to another child. So once we understand the complete story, we can better appreciate the context so that we do not judge either information or human actions too harshly and too prematurely.

Another example that illustrates a lack of context occurred on Fox News during the 2018 National Football League season. News anchors on Fox News stated that players on the Philadelphia Eagles football team were protesting the American national anthem by kneeling during the anthem instead of standing. There was a bit of a problem with this news coverage, however. As it turns out, the pictures taken of the players kneeling were done prior to the game, and the players were actually praying.

And then there's Jussie Smollett. Smollett is a gay black man and actor who gained moderate recognition playing a role on a drama series called *Empire*. Apparently, Smollett had complained to his employer that he had received a death threat in the form of a cryptic letter. When his employer maintained that there was not much to the letter, Smollett made international headlines on January 29, 2019, by becoming the alleged victim of a brutal racist and homophobic attack from two pro-Trump assailants who allegedly beat him, called him racist and homophobic slurs, poured bleach on him (to make him white), and placed a white rope noose around his neck. When the story first broke, many people were horrified by the brutality of the actions.[9] Given the context of the situation, many believed that such horrific actions were *consistent* with the values and beliefs of standard Trump supporters. However, when the Chicago Police Department began to investigate the alleged occurrence, they found out that much of Smollett's story did not make sense. As it turns out, it appears that Smollett staged the incident and had hired his gym trainers to be involved. In other words, it appeared that Smollett paid someone to treat him this way. The police superintendent, Eddie Johnson, and the mayor of Chicago, Rahm Emanuel, were outraged that such a wonton and fraudulent disregard for the law had been perpetrated. In an unusual twist, all sixteen felony charges against Smollett were dropped. Many members of the Chicago Police Department as well as Mayor Emanuel were vocally critical of the outcome, saying, "This is a whitewash of justice . . . is there no decency in this man?"[10] So what are we to think? At one point in this story, we might have been outraged at such an act against a gay black man. At another point in the story, we might be outraged at a man for pretending to be the victim of such a horrible crime. The important point to note is that once the context changes, so do our opinions. Once we learn a little more of the backstory behind the motivation for such actions—which, as the superintendent of police maintained, was Smollett's attempt to bargain for more money for his role on *Empire*—we may alter our views and beliefs regarding the injustice and brutality of such an act. Ask yourself what you now believe about Smollett. How have you come to your current understanding and belief regarding what really happened?

Smollett's plan was not all that original. For those of you born before 1970, you may be familiar with the movie *Dirty Harry* starring Clint Eastwood. In this movie, the antagonist, named Scorpio, has himself beaten up in order to try to frame Clint Eastwood's character, Detective Harry Callahan, for police brutality. Of course, in classic style, when asked about the alleged assault, Callahan responds by saying, "Anybody can tell I didn't do that to him . . . [because] he looks too damn good."

In considering more classic examples, just think of the number of times you would have experienced the importance of context in so many forms of literature, such as great works of fiction, historical dramas, television, plays, movies, and so on. For example, many of Shakespeare's plays are based on the lack of contextual information the characters have. This often leads to ironic or comedic and, sometimes, tragic events. In the final scene of *Romeo and Juliet*, our love-struck Romeo has no idea that Juliet has been drugged by Friar Lawrence, making it seem as though she is dead. Believing this to be real, Romeo consumes real poison, which eventually really kills him. When Juliet awakens from her fake death state, she sees poor Romeo, who is now really dead beside her. Overcome with grief, she drinks real poison and so really dies as well, all because of a failure to really understand context. Had Romeo known the true context of the situation in which Friar Lawrence had provided Juliet with a serum that made her appear dead, the ending could have been quite different—like in *All's Well That Ends Well*—only with a lot less death.

The importance of context cannot be overstated. Each of us owes a duty to those with whom we communicate, to ourselves, and to the very recognition of the value of critical thinking to make the effort to obtain the necessary facts, backstory, and background information, as well as the who, what, where, when, why, and how, to ensure that we have sufficiently understood the context in which those facts take place and unfold. If we can do this while at the same time recognizing the biases within others and ourselves, then both sides of an issue will have acted in a responsible and considerate manner. It is hoped that the equal and shared practice of such critical thinking skills will naturally lead to a greater sense of fairness in the interpretation, understanding, and acting on information obtained through all forms of media. Fairness and equity must prevail among rivals in order for both sides to be heard. Strict adherence to the rules of critical thinking must be abided by both sides—if not, then fair and helpful dialogue will not and cannot take place.

Since it will always be difficult to determine how much context is necessary before one chooses an opinion or a side regarding important issues, we must understand that the context surrounding information is always accepted conditionally. In other words, there is a point in one's mind where we feel justified that we have enough relevant, reliable, and sufficient information regarding a particular issue to take a position on that issue. This level of context will vary from person to person. However, we must allow everyone the same right in believing they have satisfied the contextual background of an issue.

ALWAYS HEDGE YOUR BETS WHEN CONSIDERING CONTEXT

In order to be cautious in our consideration of the context of information, we might wish to hedge our bets, as it were, by stating a conditional, or *proviso*, regarding the information itself. In other words, enough relevant, reliable, and sufficient information depends on the condition that one believes to be in possession of enough information to accurately identify the context in which that information is found. So the proper understanding of context is very much about playing fairly. You want to be sure you have interpreted the information in the best spirit of its intention. This is in keeping with the *Golden Rule of Dialogue*; that is, it is what you would expect of others with your claims. So you shall do the same for them.

So we can conditionally state that we understand context in the following ways:

1. All things considered, I currently believe . . .
2. Given what I now know, I currently believe . . .
3. Based on the information I now have, I currently believe . . .

The better we understand context, the more fairly we can consider and analyze information. Some might wonder why we should even want to play fairly. The world is a cruel place filled with people who don't play fairly. Some of them end up in jail, some of them become chief executive officers, and some become world leaders. It's easy to be cynical of a world that today seems so out of sorts. But during this Age of Immediacy, in which integrity has given way to reality TV, it is important to remember that the values of critical thinking have not budged, nor will they ever waiver from their cornerstone of fairness. Playing fairly and cooperating are the only ways in which civilized societies can keep order and respect in a world where there exist so many cheaters. The world is made up of lots of different types of people, but many of them can be broken down into two types: cooperators and cheaters. When it comes to critical thinking, if we all cooperate and play by the rules fairly, then we will all get more of what it is we truly value. However, humans are often shortsighted and stupid. They often fail to see the shortcomings of their own selfish reasoning. Be this as it may, the fact of the matter is that cooperation can also be a collective selfish act, one that produces a net greater benefit for the entire group. Critical thinking allows us to accomplish just such a feat; if we all cooperate and abide by its rules fairly, we will save considerable time, money, and energy. In so doing, we will all be better empowered to have been heard and to hear the freest ideas of thought on as many issues as are possible to discuss.

THE RULES FOR FAIR PLAY IN CRITICAL THINKING

Now that we know how to develop an argument, use different forms of reasoning, understand biases, and appreciate context, we have come to the point in the book where we need to explicitly state the rules of fair play for critical thinking:

1. *Determine and state freely your biases*—If both sides of an issue state their biases in advance, both will understand the ways in which they have filtered information and potentially affected the way they have interpreted and acted on information. This step is crucial, for it demonstrates the honest and open disclosure of what we already know: that it is impossible to live without biases. When we openly admit our biases, it increases the likelihood of being understood and allows those in disagreement to better appreciate (though perhaps not agree with) how we came to our current conclusion regarding an issue. But this requires that we perform an honest *bias check* that fairly depicts our current biases.

2. *Attain factual information*—It is incumbent on us to make every effort in the attainment of a *sufficient* amount of factual information prior to formulating a position or developing an argument on a particular issue. This fact-checking procedure must consider all information—including information that does not confirm a preestablished bias. No information should be buried if it is *relevant* to the issue at hand and has been *reliably* attained.

3. *Our current beliefs are always conditional*—When stating your position regarding a particular issue, it is important for people to know that the reason that you come down on one side rather than another is based not only on personal biases but also on

the information that is currently available to you at a given time. However, you want to make clear that your current position—however firm—is and must always be conditional; that is, it is based on information that is currently available to you. If new information develops or comes to light, there is always a possibility to alter one's current belief or position on that particular issue. So conditionals can be stated in the form "All things considered, this is what I now believe." If we do not take this conditional stance on issues, then we are dogmatists—those who believe with certainty that they cannot possibly be wrong. There is a great, inherent danger in claiming certainty on information. This book is not nearly large enough to completely cover why this is so. Suffice to say that when one is so dogmatic about their beliefs regarding a particular issue that they will not entertain the very possibility that they could be wrong, then they have stopped learning, they have stopped listening, and they will be justified in acting in accordance with their beliefs regardless of the consequences. Whether the belief system is religious or secular or political or philosophical, if dogmatism prevails, horrific actions can be justified. So as a species, we must admit that we are in possession of very little certainty about the nature of reality.

Know your brain! We should not—and cannot—allow our limbic systems to override our prefrontal cortexes on the importance of acknowledging and accepting our ignorance with humility and respect. No matter how passionate any of us might speak of our so-called certain knowledge, we must all recognize that this simply is not the case. There is not a single one of us who knows and can demonstrate that they are in possession of absolutely certain knowledge of the nature of reality. If you think that you are, then by all means demonstrate this in the form of a convincing argument—but state your biases first.

4. *Disagreement is inevitable, so present a steelman argument*—Anticipate and be prepared for eventual but inevitable disagreements on important issues. In so doing, acknowledge that the complex ways in which people can be biased is going to lead to inevitable disagreements. It is for this reason that we must make every effort to understand their point of view from within

their particular, contextual, and biased perspective. In practice, this translates to *steelmanning*: one's ability to be able to state back to their discussant a concise but accurate account of their argument that can, it is hoped, bring even greater clarity to it. Both sides should be able to reiterate back to one another an accurate account of each other's argument. This demonstrates a respect not only for the value of clarity but also for the reciprocal fairness that results from such an act.

5. *Above all, be humble*—As difficult as it may be, be humble and open to the possibility that at least on some things you could be wrong.

This last point is important, for there is nothing more alluring, hypnotic, or seductive, than the *high of feeling right*. This is a primal and ancestral urge that dwells within most of us.[11] It involves the desire for elevated status based on one's knowledge in a given field or procedural action. It activates several different types of neurotransmitters that produce a pleasurable high for the individual or group. The high of feeling right is intoxicating. You can see it in the eyes of every dogmatist who believes that they are so certain of their convictions that there is no need to consider the possibility of being in error. There are few things in this world more dangerous than a person so incredibly high on being blindly sure of themselves that they cannot fathom the possibility of being wrong. In our efforts to gain control over the conditions and constraints through which we survive as a species, those who are perceived to have the most worthy of information are valued highly within those specific groups. And whether religious or secular, gaining any form of exalted status as a result of claiming some information to be true that is then accepted widely by other members within that group creates an individual high for the leader, and the feeling of being right can also be experienced and then celebrated collectively as a group. For example, any organization that maintains privileged access to knowledge concerning the very nature of reality, such as religious institutions, will collectively maintain the truthfulness of their privileged view of the universe and themselves in it. So we must admit to ourselves and to others that as a species, the allure of feeling right and the neural payback of satisfaction that comes with it is sometimes so overwhelming that it can blind us from considering counterinformation. Information that runs counter to our most cherished beliefs often generates what is known as *cognitive dissonance*. In other words, as a species, we tend to favor very highly our own current beliefs, so we tend to pay more attention to information that proves to us or confirms that we are on the right track in believing this information. As we have seen, this is often referred to as *confirmation bias*: the act of looking only for information that confirms one's current biased views while ignoring counterfactual information. The act of acknowledging only such information because it confirms one's already established bias is known as an *echo chamber*. As long as one stays in the echo chamber, one cannot witness any contradictory or counterfactual information that might possibly raise any level of doubt in one's current beliefs. Counterfactual information to one's most cherished views can often bring about cognitive dissonance or a feeling of unease, or what the ancient skeptics called *disquietude*. In order for a person to escape this feeling of cognitive dissonance, they have various options available to them. For example, they can simply ignore it, or they can try to justify it or explain it in ways that they find satisfactory. So let us not forget that when we have discussions about important issues, many of us are going to be prone to the allure that comes with the *high of feeling right*. So we are up against a long history of biological and cultural biases that have made the feeling of being right so intoxicating and alluring. But if we could admit that we might be wrong in our views, then it opens the door for the possibility for us to change our minds should new information or evidence warrant this. So this last point speaks to one of the greatest of all human virtues: *humility*. Socrates and the ancient skeptics talked at great length about being humble in what one claims to know. So we need to heed this advice because of the dangers of dogmatism and cocksureness. But humility takes time and practice and does not come easily for many. So let us at least come to some agreement regarding how little we actually know about the certainty of our convictions. To remind us of this, consider the ancient Indian parable of the four blind men trying to determine what an elephant is.

Context is key. To conclude our discussion on the importance of context, let us remember to be careful when interpreting information to make sure we have established enough background information—in terms of relevance, reliability, and sufficiency—to be able to acknowledge the context in which the information is being presented. By understanding how our biases affect our judgments, by considering the

Figure 3.2. Context and Judgment

amount of information we have attained along with the context in which it is presented, and by abiding by the five rules for fair play in critical thinking, we can go a long way toward increasing the likelihood of a fair forum for discussion, which will ultimately lead to more effective and successful communication for all parties.

· 4 ·

Breathe from Your Diagram

$\mathcal{N}$ow that we know the ABCs of critical thinking—that is, we know what arguments are and the types of reasoning used to formulate them, we know how biological and cultural biases influence the way in which we interpret information in the construction of arguments, and we know how important context is in attaining reliable, relevant, and sufficient background information—it's time to learn a very important and practical skill: diagramming arguments.

Diagramming arguments is perhaps the most technical—and potentially the most boring—of the critical thinking skills within the skill set. But it is arguably (pun intended) one of the most important. Diagramming arguments allows us to visually see what an argument looks like by carefully diagramming its structure. This skill allows us to see what our and others' argumentative houses look like. This, in turn, puts us in a better position to consider the strength of their premises. Diagramming an argument also extends on the value of fairness within critical thinking because it allows us to be able to express our interpretation of another person's argument in the best possible light in order to most accurately and fairly depict the intention of their argument. Once we are able to identify the structure of a person's argument from their overall conclusion (or roof) to their supporting premises (or walls), we are in a better position to understand the manner in which they have satisfied or failed to satisfy the foundational criteria of consistency, simplicity, relevance, reliability, and sufficiency. So it is a skill that literally allows us to visually see another person's or our own argument. Diagramming also allows us to focus particularly on the key components of a person's argument. It does this by weeding out the most important premises from what can be called *noise*. Noise may provide setting or context—"It was a dark and stormy night"—but may not be directly relevant to the overall argument itself. Diagramming simply allows us to be better prepared in distinguishing between the premises and the conclusion.

Whether you realize it or not, arguments are everywhere. They exist whenever you watch television, surf online, ride a bus, drive in a car, walk on the street, dream, have sex, go to the washroom, or gossip. If you have ever gotten a speeding ticket, dealt with a lawyer, went to school, played sports, or committed a crime, you are inundated with arguments. They're all around you every day of your life—whether you are aware of them or not. Remember that all it takes to construct an argument is to have one premise and a conclusion. That's it. Most arguments are much more involved and complex. However, we cannot deny the fact that they exist in various forms throughout our lifetimes.

Whenever you see members of Congress or Parliament engaged in discussion, they are stating arguments for why they believe their ideas should be the ones that should be adopted by society. Whenever you have discussions with family, friends, coworkers, or complete strangers, you will find that you are presenting and exchanging ideas in the form of arguments. Even if you just talk about the weather, you may be stating conclusions regarding how much you enjoy or dislike it and then subsequently stating why.

The most obvious arguments we are confronted with on a daily basis come in the form of advertisements. With advertisements, the conclusion is always or usually always hidden: buy this product. So once we can determine what the conclusion is, we can then go about determining what the supporting premises are and whether or not we believe they have satisfied the foundational criteria of consistency, simplicity, relevance, reliability, and sufficiency. So when you come across an argument, you must first determine what the conclusion is. After that, what follows will be the premises and perhaps noise. To determine the conclusion, you must ask yourself what you believe the person's overall point is that they're trying to make.

At this point, we need to take a minute to become familiar with some abbreviations that stand for the various parts of an argument.

Basic premises are abbreviated as a capital P. And the conclusion is abbreviated as a capital C. Arrows are then used to show the connection between the premises and the conclusion.

For example, consider the following argument:

Matthew McConaughey drives a Lincoln Nautilus car. He was driving one long before he got paid to drive one. I think Matthew McConaughey is a trustworthy guy. So I'm going to buy a Lincoln Nautilus.

In this example, there are three premises:

P1: Matthew McConaughey drives a Lincoln Nautilus.
P2: Matthew McConaughey drove one before he was paid to drive one.
P3: Matthew McConaughey is a trustworthy person.

Each premise provides a separate reason to support my conclusion that I will buy a Lincoln Nautilus. For a diagram of this argument, see figure 4.1.

So the three basic premises, P1, P2, and P3, are the supports for the conclusion, C, just as walls support the roof. This is called a *simple argument*—in other words, it is not extremely complex. There is no noise to separate from the premises or conclusion. In terms of considering the foundational criteria, all three premises appear to be internally consistent. That is, my admiration for McConaughey's acting ability is proof enough for me that he would make good choices in cars. However, we cannot determine the external consistency of the premises because he does not tell me much technical information about the vehicle, such as gas mileage, performance, steering, and price. The premises appear to satisfy the criterion of simplicity, and all of them appear to be relevant in support of the conclusion. But we are currently unable to determine

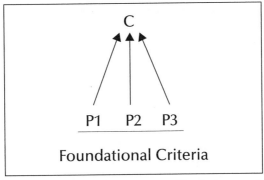

Figure 4.1. Diagram Components (Simple Argument)

either the reliability or the sufficiency of the premises because we simply have no idea yet about the performance qualities of the vehicle.

There is a second type of premises, called *main premises*, abbreviated as MP. As we saw above, a premise (P) is a support for a conclusion (C), but it can also support a main premise (MP). Consider the following example stated by Bradley Coutts:

> Bernadette Doyle is experienced, courageous, and honest. These are all the types of qualities that make a good mayor. That's why I think you should vote for Bernadette Doyle.

In this argument, the conclusion (or roof) is that people should vote for Bernadette Doyle to become mayor. But unlike the first example, this argument contains a main premise. Can you spot it? It's the claim that her experience, courage, and honesty are the types of qualities that make a good mayor. For a diagram of this argument, see figure 4.2.

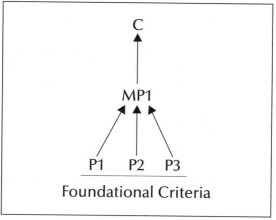

Figure 4.2.   Diagram Components (Complex Argument)

THE HIDDEN CONCLUSION

Just as there are two types of premises—P and MP—there are two types of conclusions, abbreviated as C and HC. The conclusion can either be stated (C) or hidden (HC). As we saw in the example above, when a conclusion is stated, it is labeled as C. But when it is unstated, it is labeled as HC. As we have seen, the most common arguments that have hidden conclusions are advertisements. As we saw above, the conclusion to most advertisements is generally the same: buy this product. But this is rarely stated in an ad. Instead, advertisements use other techniques in their arguments to try to convince you to buy their product. And if they convince you—for whatever reasons—you may buy their product, and they can make money.

Now that we have visually seen how the structure of arguments can be drawn, we need to consider how we can easily spot premises and conclusions. In all arguments—whether written or verbal—we are sometimes given clues as to where these are. So we must search for what are called *indicator words*. As the name suggests, they *indicate* to us where, precisely, the premises and conclusions can be found. Here is a partial list of both types:

Conclusion-Indicators

therefore	we may infer that
hence	*I conclude that*
thus	which shows/reveals that
so	*which means that*
ergo	establishes
then	implies
consequently	proves that
as a result	justifies
follows	supports

Premise-Indicators

since	the reason(s) is (are)
as indicated by	*for*
if	*as*
because	given that

The indicator words that appear in italics are the most commonly used in everyday language. It should be noted that not all types of arguments will contain these terms because they can be used in ways that indicate neither premises nor conclusions. However, it is often the case that they do indicate the specific parts of an argument, and learning this distinction will take time and practice.

FORMAL GUIDELINES FOR DIAGRAMMING A WRITTEN ARGUMENT

The first step in diagramming a written argument is to find the conclusion. If it is stated clearly, we underline it. If you're not sure what the overall point or conclusion is, it may be hidden. But if it is stated clearly, underline it. What then remains will be the remaining premises and perhaps some noise. In the next step, we circle any words that indicate where the conclusion is and where the premises are. This will help us with the third step, which is to place square brackets around what you believe to be individual premises. Then determine if they are basic premises (P) or a main premise (MP) and number them accordingly: P1, P2, MP1, and so on.

In the Bradley Coutts example above, he maintained that

P1[Bernadette Doyle is experienced], P2[courageous], and P3[honest]. MP1[These are all the types of qualities that make a good mayor]. That's why I think <u>you should vote for Bernadette Doyle</u>.

The next step involves the construction of a legend. You must write out each of the premises, the main premises, and the conclusion. For example, in the argument above, the components of Bradley's argument would be placed in a legend in the following manner:

P1 = Bernadette Doyle is experienced
P2 = She is courageous
P3 = She is honest
MP1 = These are all the types of qualities that make a good mayor
C = You should vote for Bernadette Doyle

The purpose of the legend is to make sure we understand the argument and can state it in the manner in which it was intended. In other words, it allows us to treat the speaker's argument fairly. This will allow you to faithfully and accurately represent what you believe to be the intention of the person making the argument. Sometimes it will be necessary to apply what is called the *principle of charity* with some of the premises. In other words, if a person uses slang or jargon, you need to present what you honestly believe was their intended meaning. For example, if someone states a premise that a politician is "out of his mind," this needs to be translated to read that they are "misguided" or "not thinking straight." In the legend, we keep an eye out for phrases containing double negatives, such as "ain't got no" (as well as slang, personal assaults, and so on), in order to reflect the person's argument in its best possible light. By doing so, you are *playing fair* by interpreting and representing their intention as accurately as possible, which—in keeping with the *Golden Rule of dialogue*—is exactly what you would expect to be done with your argument.

After we have completed a legend of the argument, we can depict its structure. A diagram of Bradley's argument is given in figure 4.3.

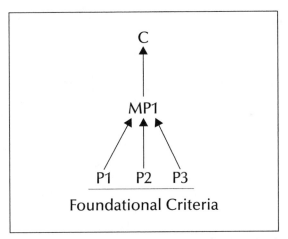

Figure 4.3. Diagram Components (Complex Argument)

So let's review. The best way to ensure that you understand another person's argument is to physically draw out its structure. Here is a basic checklist for diagramming arguments:

1. Determine the overall point or conclusion that the person is trying to make. If it is a written argument, start by underlining

the conclusion (C). If the conclusion is not clearly stated, it is probably hidden (HC).

2. Consider whether indicator words have been used. If so, circle them.

3. Place square brackets around and number the various basic or main premises.

4. Create a legend and be charitable in adjusting any wording of their premises if necessary.

5. Build a house with the conclusion on top, premises supporting, and criteria as the foundation.

COMPLEX ARGUMENTS

Keep in mind that the examples above are called *simple* arguments. Most arguments we experience are much longer and far more *complex*. This is why it is so important to be able to diagram them. It allows us to better understand them in terms of their structure. Consider this complex argument:

We have got to close down Guantanamo Bay detention camp. First, the costs to the United States are staggeringly high. One report estimates as much as $5 billion has been spent on this detention camp by U.S. tax dollars. At this rate, we will never recover our costs. Second, the information from the prisoners has not been very helpful with ending terrorism. With the use of torture strategies, the United States has damaged its reputation. And through the increased statements of denying that torture has been used, our citizens have lost confidence in their government. And there have been far too many "accidental" deaths caused by so-called resistance to cooperate. And then there is the fact that the so-called War on Terror is largely an unwinnable war. You never know if you've won such a war because terrorist acts continue to happen. And this is happening in other countries as well. Because the war on terror is unwinnable, we should get our troops out of there as soon as possible. The men behind bars have been treated brutally. And because of this, morale is at an all-time low. This is now the longest war in U.S. history. The news media don't help morale much either; they keep showing images of how often Gitmo continues to fail in its purpose. (Trinity Gibson, Lethbridge, AB)

To diagram this argument, it is going to take a little more time and patience. But we use the same techniques as were used in the simpler arguments. Just remember to follow the checklist. In this argument, Trinity Gibson wants to convince us that the U.S. government should shut down Guantanamo Bay detention camp. When we ask ourselves why she would want us to believe this, we can see a number of basic and main premises offered. The first main premise is the costs to U.S. taxpayers. She supports this with some basic premises stating how much it is costing the U.S. taxpayers and the unlikelihood of recovering the costs. Her second main premise is that the information from the prisoners has not been very helpful with ending terrorism. Her basic premises to support this include the damage caused to the international reputation of the United States, a loss of confidence in the government, and the result of too many "accidental" deaths. Her third main premise is that the so-called War on Terror is essentially an unwinnable war. This is supported by her premise that we cannot tell when a war on terror has been won because terrorist acts continue to happen. And this is further supported by her claim that similar wars on terror are being experienced in other countries as well. This is further reason to bring the U.S. troops out of Guantanamo Bay. Finally, the last major premise stating the brutal treatment of the prisoners has morale at an all-time low. This is supported by the claim that the length of the war is another reason that morale is low, and the media are implicated in contributing to this depiction of low morale.

Regardless of whether you happen to agree with Gibson's argument for the closing down of Guantanamo Bay detention camp, your concern right now lies with the structure of her argument. When we diagram her argument, it looks like this:

We have got to close down Guantanamo Bay Detention Camp. First, MP1[the costs to the United States are staggeringly high] One report estimates ^{P1}[as much as $5 billion has been spent on this war by U.S. tax dollars]. At this rate, ^{P2}[we will never recover our costs]. Second, ^{MP2}[the information from the prisoners has not been very helpful with ending terrorism]. ^{P3}[With the use of torture strategies, the United States has damaged its reputation]. And ^{P4}[through the increased statements of denying that torture has been used, our citizens have lost confidence in their government]. (And) P5[there have been far too many "accidental" deaths caused by so-called resistance to cooperate]. (And)hen there is the fact that MP3 [the so-called War on Terror is largely an unwinnable war]. P6[You never know if you've won such a war because terrorist acts continue to happen].(And) P7[this is happening in other countries as well].(Because) P8[the war on terror is unwinnable, we should get our troops out of there as soon as possible]. P9[The men behind bars have been treated brutally].(And because)of this, MP4[morale is at an all-time low]. P10[This is now the longest war in U.S. history]. P11[The news media don't help morale much either; they keep showing images of how often Gitmo continues to fail in its purpose]. (Trinity Gibson, Lethbridge, AB)

The legend would look like this:

C = The U.S. government should close down Guantanamo Bay Detention Camp.

MP1 = The costs to the United States are staggeringly high.

P1 = As much as $5 billion has been spent on this war by U.S. tax dollars.

P2 = The United States will never recover the costs.

MP2 = The information from the prisoners has not been very helpful with ending terrorism.

P3 = With the use of torture strategies, the United States has damaged its reputation.

P4 = Through the increased statements of denying that torture has been used, our citizens have lost confidence in their government.

P5 = There have been far too many "accidental" deaths caused by so-called resistance to cooperate. Translation: The lives of prisoners are being lost but under mysterious circumstances.

MP3 = The so-called War on Terror is largely an unwinnable war.

P6 = You never know if you've won such a war because terrorist acts continue to happen.

P7 = This is happening in other countries as well.

P8 = The war on terror is unwinnable, we should get our troops out of there as soon as possible.

P9 = The men behind bars have been treated brutally.

MP4 = Morale at Guantanamo Bay is at an all-time low.

P10 = This is now the longest war in U.S. history.

P11 = The news media don't help U.S. morale because they keep showing images of how often Gitmo continues to fail in its purpose.

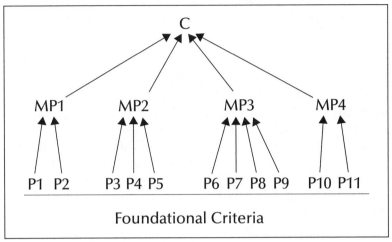

Figure 4.4. Trinity Gibson Argument

As you can see in figure 4.4, Gibson's argument is rather complex. But she has stated it in a way that is relatively easy for us to follow and understand because there is very little noise. Many arguments are much more complex than this and would require a significant amount of time and energy to diagram. Some arguments are much simpler. For now, the best practice for diagramming is found online on blogs or in local newspapers or Internet letters to the editor. Usually, short letters and blogs about various issues provide plenty of information with which you can practice your diagramming techniques. If you want to know if you are using these techniques properly, feel free to connect with me online at http://www.criticalthinkingsolutions.ca.

Let's now consider an actual argument that has been stated in the public domain. This one comes from President Donald Trump on March 20, 2019, at a rally in Ohio:

Hillary wanted to put up wind, wind! If you have a windmill any-where near your house, congratulations . . . your house just went down 75 percent in value. And they say, the noise causes cancer, you tell me that one okay [gesturing with his hand and making a whirring sound]. The thing makes noise; it's so noisy. And of course, it's like a graveyard for birds. If you love birds, you'd never want to walk under a windmill, 'cause it's a very sad, sad sight. It's like a cemetery. You'd be doing wind! Windmills! Weeeeee! And if it doesn't blow, you can forget about television for that night. "Darling, I want to watch television." "I'm sorry, the wind isn't blowing." I know a lot about wind. I know a lot about wind.[1]

So how would we faithfully diagram such an argument? Remember, begin by trying to establish the overall point or conclusion that Trump is trying to make. It seems fairly obvious that he is not thrilled about wind power. But he never states it explicitly. We must simply infer this from his many criticisms and jokes regarding wind power. So the hidden conclusion would be something like "Windmill power is bad." It is not stated; it is insinuated or implied, and we are left to infer this from his list of the bad things that happen from windmill power. Okay, so wind power is bad. What are his reasons or premises for stating this? We can diagram his argument the following way:

P1[Hillary wanted to put up wind, wind! P2[(If)you have a windmill anywhere near your house, congratulations . . . your house just went down 75% in value.] P3(And)they say, the noise causes cancer], you tell me that one okay (gesturing with his hand in making a whirring sound). P4[The thing makes noise; it's so noisy.](And)of course, P5[it's like a graveyard for birds. (If)you love birds, you'd never want to walk under a windmill, 'cause it's a very sad, sad sight. It's like a cemetery.] You'd be doing wind! Windmills! Weeeeee! P6(And)if it doesn't blow, you can forget about television for that night.] "Darling, I want to watch television." "I'm sorry, the wind isn't blowing." P7[I know a lot about wind. I know a lot about wind.]

The legend would like this:

P1 = Democratic presidential candidate Hillary Clinton was in favor of wind power.

P2 = Wind turbines cause the depreciation of property values.

P3 = The noise of wind turbines causes cancer.

P4 = Wind turbines are very noisy.

P5 = Wind turbines kill large numbers of birds.

P6 = When there is no wind, there is no electrical power.

P7 = Donald Trump is an authority on wind.

C = Wind turbines are bad.

You must remember that, as bad as you might believe this argument to be, you cannot let your emotions or your political biases affect the way in which you diagram it. You must faithfully and accurately represent the intent of the argument in the spirit in which it was stated. Otherwise, you are not being fair to the person making the argument. If you disagree with the argument, that's fine. But you must not misrepresent the intention of the premises or conclusion. You will have plenty of time to analyze and criticize the argument after you have faithfully stated and diagrammed it:

> Noise:
> You tell me that one okay [gesturing with his hand in making a whirring sound].
> You'd be doing wind! Windmills! Weeeeee!
> "Darling, I want to watch television." "I'm sorry, the wind isn't blowing."

The noise does provide some context because it demonstrates a tone of mockery. In other words, President Trump is implying that wind power is such a bad idea that it deserves to be ridiculed along with those who might be in favor of it.

With the noise removed, President Trump's argument can be diagrammed, as shown in figure 4.5.

Now that we have faithfully represented the intent of President Trump's argument, we can consider its strengths and weaknesses. Although we will look at how to consider evidence and errors in logic and reasoning in the next two chapters, what we can say so far about this argument is that it appeals to both opinion and facts. P1 and P7 are purely Trump's opinion. He disagrees with Hillary Clinton's political ideology in P1, and claiming to be an authority on wind in P7 is purely his own opinion. But notice how the middle premises—from P2 to P6—are all fact based. When someone makes factual claims, that means

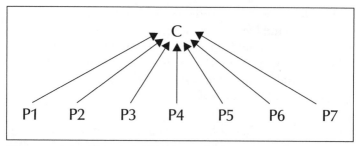

Figure 4.5.   President Donald Trump's 'Wind' Argument

that the claims are empirical. In other words, we can literally check to see if they're true. It would be like if I said, "You know, cocoa comes from coconuts." We can check to see if this statement is true; that is, does it consistently measure up to the facts of the external world? As it turns out, no, cocoa does not come from coconuts at all. A coconut is a drupe, or stone fruit, which commonly grows on palm trees, whereas cocoa is a bean that comes from cocoa trees.

So let's consider the factual content of President Trump's five premises from P2 to P6. First, in P2, he states that windmills cause the depreciation of property values. First of all, he is really referring to wind turbines; windmills were quaint but small constructions used mainly in the milling of grain. When we ask two important critical thinking questions—"Why?" and "How does he know this?"—we find the evidence to be somewhat lacking. Depending on your source, it turns out that Trump is correct; that is, having wind turbines on your property will reduce its value. But the figure is not 75 percent. From the sources I was able to access, the figure comes in at anywhere between 0 and 35 percent.[2] So in this case, he is somewhat correct but inaccurate and somewhat exaggerated.

His third premise is an interesting claim: that the noise of windmills causes cancer. So let's check the facts. What evidence is there to support such a claim? When we do some research, we find that a 2014 report from the National Institutes of Health[3] considered research from approximately sixty scientific peer-reviewed articles on the subject and concluded that the electromagnetic fields, shadow flicker, audible noise, and low-frequency noise (infrasound) created by wind turbines are not likely to affect human health and do not cause cancer. They may be annoying, but they are not unhealthy.

As for his fourth premise—that windmills are very noisy—we find that there is some truth to this claim. However, noise in this respect seems to be a relative term. Lots of things cause noise: traffic, school yards, construction, and so on. The question to consider now is whether the noise is so excessive that it cannot be tolerated.

President Trump's fifth premise states that wind turbines kill large numbers of birds. What are large numbers? Let's go to the facts. According to one study,[4] between 140,000 and 328,000 birds are killed each year by wind turbines in the greater United States. To put some perspective (or context) onto this issue, it is estimated that approximately 6.8 million birds are killed each year in the United States by cell and radio towers, and between 1.4 and 3.7 billion birds die as a result of cats.[5] So, yes, Trump is correct in stating that wind turbines do kill large numbers of birds. But he ignored the fact that this is significantly less than other causes and that measures are being taken to reduce bird fatalities by wind turbines; for example, some companies are now using radar and GPS to detect when birds are nearby so that they can be stopped before birds can fly into them.

In regard to President Trump's sixth premise—that when there is no wind, there is no electrical power—it would appear that this is simply factually wrong. A turbine can either transmit electrical power directly or store it. In the case of wind turbines, electrical energy is stored in batteries until it is needed. So the "windmills" do not have to be turning in order for people to access and utilize electricity.

The importance of diagramming cannot be overstated. All arguments can be diagrammed in this way. Some are much simpler, but many are far more complex. Every argument can be diagrammed if we take the time and have the patience to consider its structure. Now that we have considered the ways in which it is easier for us to see the structure of an argument, it is time to consider the *evidence* of those premises.

Evidence

Show Me the Money!

$\mathcal{W}$hen we consider the value of someone's argument by considering how well their premises satisfy the universal foundational criteria of consistency, relevance, reliability, simplicity, and sufficiency, there are often two main questions that emerge: "Why should I believe you?" and "How do you know that what you claim is true?" So we are really questioning the methods and reasons (or premises) for why someone believes what they do. Quite often, we expect some form of proof or evidence as support for their premises.

Because there are many different types of claims that we and others make every day, some require very little evidence to convince someone of our views. For example, when you ask someone how they're doing and they reply by saying, "I'm fine," we generally don't demand of them supporting evidence for such a claim. This is simply small talk or commentary. Other claims, however, require considerably more evidence. As we saw with examples of extraordinary claims like the existence of aliens, that the moon landing didn't take place, or that Bigfoot exists, these would require considerably more evidence. In determining the sufficiency of evidence, use the Sagan principle: "Extraordinary claims require extraordinary evidence." Remember that the more spectacular or extraordinary the claim, the more convincing or greater the evidence will need to be to support such a conclusion.

Evidence is often required to demonstrate to someone that your argument is justified in being held. But the burden of proof in convincing someone that they should be convinced of an argument always lies with the person who's making the claim. So it follows, then, that when

Figure 5.1

presenting evidence to support a claim, one must satisfy several of the universal foundational criteria, namely, consistency, relevance, reliability, and sufficiency. The foundational criterion of simplicity might also hold as well. For example, a simpler explanation generally abides by the KISS principle (Keep It Simple Stupid). In complying with Occam's razor and not adding premises to an argument beyond what is necessary to convince someone, simplicity is often—though not always—a significant criterion for the acceptance of evidence. As with the Sagan principle, the stronger the claim, the greater the burden of proof and the more convincing the evidence is going to have to be.

Whenever anyone makes a claim that requires considerable proof, you have a right to state, "Show me the evidence! Show me the money!" For example, if you present convincing evidence in support of your premises, then I would have to agree. To be a responsible critical thinker, I will follow wherever the evidence leads me. But if you don't have evidence to support your conclusion, why should I believe you? Why should I do your work for you? You should want to make it easy for people to believe you; this means that you have some homework to do. You have to support your premises with evidence that satisfies the universal foundational criterion of *acceptability*. Otherwise, we have no real compelling reasons to accept your argument.

The importance of proper evidence cannot be overstated. Historically, there have been many writers and scholars who have praised the importance of evidence. One of them was an Englishman by the name of William Kingdon Clifford. He was a nineteenth-century mathematician, and his basic philosophy can be reduced to a very interesting statement: "It is wrong always, everywhere, and for everyone, to believe anything upon insufficient evidence."[1] Here, Clifford is referring to the importance of the universal foundational criterion of *sufficiency*. In other words, Clifford stressed the great importance of having *enough* evidence to convince someone. But how do we determine when there is enough evidence? Conviction will vary between people, but there generally are ways of determining this. For example, what would be sufficient evidence to convince me that Bigfoot exists? You can't just show me big-footed prints in the snow or bad video footage of what could be just about anything. You would need to supply substantial evidence, such as a body. If you showed me a Sasquatch body—dead or alive—and mammalian biologists confirmed that it was, indeed, a Sasquatch, then I would *have* to believe in their existence.

With regard to the importance of evidence, there was another gentleman, a Scotsman by the name of David Hume, who said, "Wise people proportion themselves to the evidence." This means that you should not just believe anything for any reason, especially if those premises require evidence in order to have sufficient support. Hume's statement is a precursor to Sagan's principle. The two are referring to the proportionality of belief with regard to the evidence. Right now, I have no reason to believe that Bigfoot (or any Sasquatch) exists. I have proportioned myself to the evidence or, in this case, the lack thereof. Should the evidence change, I may need to re-proportion myself and change my disbelief in such creatures. But until that happens—and I'm not holding my breath—I will continue to proportion myself to the lack of evidence and continue to disbelieve in the existence of Sasquatches.

Now, whenever we make a claim, a statement, or an argument, our premises are intended to support our intended conclusion. It is often the case that our premises require various forms or types of evidence. So whenever you make any claim, the burden of proof lies with you to support it. Others shouldn't have to do your work for you. If you claim that aliens walk among us, fine. Let's see them. Let's see your evidence. I will believe you if I find the evidence compelling enough to believe. So you need to provide the evidence to make somebody believe something to be true. You can't just say, "Well, you can't prove it's *not* true." To do so would be to commit the argumentum ad ignorantium fallacy—an error in reasoning we're going to look at more closely in the next chapter. If you make a claim—any claim—the onus of responsibility lies with you to demonstrate why other people should believe it. If it is an extraordinary claim, the greater the burden of proof will be on you in support of it and the more convincing the evidence is going to have to be. So varying types of evidence can be supplied in support of a conclusion, and various types of methods can be used to measure the effectiveness of those types of evidence. At this point, we are going to consider four different types of evidence: anecdotal evidence, legal evidence, intuition, and scientific evidence.

ANECDOTAL EVIDENCE

The first type is the most basic. It is called *anecdotal evidence*. An anecdote is a personal experience. It is usually limited to one individual having one particular experience at one particular time. The reason that this type of evidence is problematic is because it often leads to improper generalizations. Consider the following example. Imagine a person; let's call him Dick. Let's imagine that Dick believes that all women are bad drivers. So Dick is in possession of an already established, already confirmed bias that no matter who the driver is, if it's a woman, then it follows that she's a bad driver. Now let's imagine that Dick is driving on a busy interstate highway and that he is suddenly and unexpectedly cut off by another car. If the driver of the car turns out to be a woman, then Dick's anecdotal evidence of a single experience confirms his already established bias against women drivers. However, should the driver turn out to be a man, Dick might simply ignore this information (or data) because it does not confirm his already established bias. What started his bias in the first place might have been due to a small number of instances where examples of bad driving happened to have been done by women. When maintaining such obvious confirmed biases, don't be a Dick. Try to be a little more open-minded and accept that anecdotal evidence of this nature is neither warranted nor acceptable.

When something happens to us personally, it can leave a big impression on us. So we naturally use those experiences as guides for our future behavior. However, anecdotal, or personal, experiences can often lead to unfair generalizations known in critical thinking as the *fallacy of generalization*. This particular error in reasoning is often how sexism, racism, ageism, and all forms and sorts of "isms" result through improper generalizations based on personal, individual, anecdotal experiences. So the idea that vaccinations cause autism in children is an example of an error in reasoning by personal anecdotal evidence by a single person—namely, Jenny McCarthy. McCarthy observed signs of autism in her son after being vaccinated, and then she concluded (by means of Google) that the vaccines *had* to have caused the symptoms in her child. This is extremely flawed reasoning. Simply because one effect occurred does not necessarily mean that one of the causes that came before it was the actual reason for its occurrence. Consider another example, one that involves a personal experience in dining. Let's say a friend of yours tells you not to eat at, say, Betty's Kitchen again because they became extremely ill after eating there. How would you know that it was the food at Betty's Kitchen and not that from another restaurant? Or from their own cooking? Or from some type of stomach bug they contracted twenty-four hours earlier? It may be the case that your friend was food-poisoned at Betty's Kitchen. But there would have to be a more extensive investigation providing more solid evidence to convince us that the precise cause of your friend's sickness originated at Betty's Kitchen. The same can be said for personal preference. For example, if you saw a movie recently that you didn't particularly like, you might tell people that it's not very good and that they shouldn't waste their money by going to see it. But these are largely just your individual opinions. We must always be on our guard against the temptation that simply because we personally believe something to be true does not necessarily make it factual.

Now, having said that, there are ways in which we can come to solid conclusions that create proper generalizations based on single episodes. For example, when a child touches a hot stove, they will learn immediately from the one incident that they shouldn't do that again. The saying "Once bitten, twice shy" comes into effect when we experience potentially dangerous situations. So there are times when one single example of anecdotal evidence is sufficient to support a conclusion.

However, they are often the exception to the rule. So we must become aware of when anecdotal instances provide the means for generalizing and especially when they do not. The standard rule for determining this involves statistically significant numbers—in other words, when we have enough anecdotal evidence by large enough groups of people, generalizations can be made. A good example of this collective form of anecdotal events occurred in the treatment of cardiac patients. Doctors were giving their heart patients a drug to help thin their blood and ease the likelihood of heart problems. Over time, the patients started to report common side effects, namely, penile erections. This serendipitous effect of the drug Viagra led to one of the biggest discoveries in pharmaceutical history, and it began with anecdotal evidence of individual patients telling their cardiologists about the side effects of Viagra. One can just imagine how cardiologists began to realize the cause of this collective side effect.

LEGAL EVIDENCE

In terms of a second form of evidence, we can look at legal evidence, legal testimonies, eyewitness accounts, and so on. People in a court of law swear under oath that the information they are providing is true. In many cases, lawyers will try to show why testimonials for their side should be valued while testimonies for the other side should not. Keep in mind that the basis for legal testimony basically rests on the assumption that the person providing the information or evidence is not lying and has agreed to swear an oath that the information that they are providing is the truth, the whole truth, and nothing but the truth. So it is based on that assumption that what they are saying is in fact the truth and that the purpose of testifying under oath is an attempt to ensure that the information being provided is truthful and accurate. Of course, the problem with this is that they could simply be lying. Swearing on a Bible or any other type of book does not guarantee that a person will not lie under oath. So elevating the importance of evidence offered in a legal context by penalty of perjury does not guarantee that a person will provide factually true information. So we need to guard ourselves in terms of what counts in a court of law. The prosecution attorneys for the O.J. Simpson case produced a mountain of evidence that would have convinced any judge in any court in the United States that Simpson was indeed guilty of two murders. What the truth is and how court decisions eventually arise are all too often two entirely different things. Let us never forget that Simpson walked away a free man from having killed two people: Nicole Brown and Ronald Goldman. Remember their names, for they should stand as a testament to the flawed nature of providing true legal evidence.

INTUITION

Another form of evidence that people often use in support of their premises is intuition. It appears in various forms, for example, "I didn't walk down that dark alley because I felt it might be dangerous," or "I didn't purchase a car from that salesman even though it seemed like a good deal at the time. There was just something about him that I didn't like." These intuitive approaches to evidence come from personal feelings about specific situations that are triggered by cues or behavioral patterns that elicit emotional responses within us. They're sometimes referred to as "hunches." We often get these gut feelings about certain issues, but there are problems with this type of evidence. They are sometimes right, but they are often wrong, and there is no way to personally regulate intuitive feelings. So what you intuitively feel about something, someone, or some piece of information might be the exact opposite of what others are feeling. So who's right? How could we possibly measure this type of evidence? It should come as little surprise, then, that intuitive evidence is the least justifiable because of its very nature. In other words, we can't measure hunches. They are just what people feel. We have to be very careful in guarding against this type of evidence; we can't let our feelings get the best of us.

Although hunches cannot yet be measured accurately, there is some very interesting work being conducted and developed in microbiology and physiology that examines the relationship between the human stomach and the brain. Known as the gut–brain connection, scientists at various universities worldwide are discovering that our stomachs are really a type of second brain. And there is a direct connection between biota—the thousands of species of microbes in our stomachs—and the operation of our brains. The stomach and the brain can influence each other through the nervous system (e.g., the vagus nerve) as well as the immune system. Known as the microbiome, our guts house some 10,000 or so species of microbes that are involved in a complex array not only for digestion but also for communication to other systems within the body. So it is possible to imagine that at some point in the future, scientists might be able to know more about what is going on at the level of our so-called gut feelings. In this way, the evidence we find compelling through our intuitions may lie within the realms of the medical sciences. In fact, I will go so far as to make a prediction that better understanding the human biome will be the most groundbreaking and interesting research for the next fifty to one hundred years. The more we can understand the connections and relationships of complex systems within our bodies, the better we will be able to treat diseases common to those systems.

SCIENTIFIC EVIDENCE

The fourth and final form of evidence is the most important and the most objectively reliable: scientific evidence. This type of evidence involves claims about our understanding of the cause-and-effect relationships of the natural world. They require that we produce physical, empirical evidence to indicate that we are on the right track in understanding how the world works. Earlier, we saw that induction, or inductive reasoning, is the hallmark of scientific investigation. This means that when we look at some particular behavior in the world and we observe that it repeatedly occurs over and over again and under similar circumstances, we then conclude that it is likely to behave the same way again in the future. Now, it has always been quite striking to me how few people in the world actually know how science works. The basis for all scientific inquiry involves a systematic method of inquiry, proposal, discovery, and consideration. The scientific method of inquiry should be taught in all schools at very early stages so that we can better appreciate what is actually going on when scientists make claims. This type of evidence works because when we look at various phenomena in the world—like the effects of gravity—and then observe that they repeatedly occur the same way under the same conditions over and over again, we can then conclude that they are likely to behave the same way in the future. So this type of evidence satisfies very well the foundational criterion of consistency. Many people do not realize it, but we use the scientific method in our lives all the time.

But before we delve into the scientific method, we need to better understand why scientific evidence is so important and how we attain it. Science touches every part of our lives, so we need to more clearly appreciate this relationship.

THE INFLUENCE OF SCIENCE

To illustrate just how much science influences our lives, I want you to consider some examples. Are you now reading this sentence by artificial light or natural light (or a little of both)? If you are using the former, do you have some comprehension as to how the electricity gets to where you are? If you are using the latter, are you aware of the thermonuclear processes that go on in any star that transfer (fuse) matter into energy according to Einstein's formula $E = mc^2$? Do you realize that in creating electricity, the main concern is the production of steam? That's right, boiling water is the single most important feature in the creation of electricity. Why boiling water? Because boiling water creates the steam needed to create enough pressure to turn the huge turbines (really huge electromagnets), which create the massive amounts of electricity that can then be distributed throughout various communities, municipalities, cities, and so on. *How* that steam is created is the interesting question.

So far, there are two methods that work pretty well: coal burning and nuclear fission. There are downsides to both, with which you are probably familiar. *If* we could come up with a better solution for creating electricity, *then* we would be less likely to create either so much pollution and carbon dioxide emissions from burning fossil fuel or so much nuclear waste. But we all like our electricity, don't we? I could not have written this book as easily without it. There are hundreds of things we would be unable to do without it. Just use your imagination for a moment and consider a day without electricity. Forget about waking up with a radio alarm clock or your cell phone; don't reach for the light switch; don't use the toaster; you no longer have a refrigerator but instead an icebox: if it's summer, good luck keeping things cool, including yourself—no fans or air conditioning; if it's winter, forget about using the furnace (better get some wood); forget about laundry with the washer and dryer (better get the washtub and washboard); no television; no stereos; no telephones; no computers; no planes, trains, or automobiles. Your entire life would change. How did we discover and develop electricity? This is a rather long story that we need not get into here. The point is that science, scientific methodology, and those people with creative minds and strong wills were responsible for its invention, distribution, and use.

The same can be said about our understanding of the sun, space, other stars, planets, galaxies, and so on. Many people have no idea what $E = mc^2$ actually means. But this is not surprising. It's not as though we need to know this information to order a meal at a restaurant, rent a car, or ride a bike. This knowledge seems somewhat abstract and removed from the day-to-day happenings of our lives. The sun continues to shine whether we know this information or not. Yet there is something fundamentally important about this equation. Einstein possessed the insight that allowed him to see that matter and energy are the same thing—only in different forms. In his famous equation, E refers to energy, and energy is equivalent to m (the mass of something) multiplied by c (the speed of light) squared.[2] The transformation of even a small amount of mass (like fusing atoms) releases an enormous amount of energy. What happens in space is that, over periods of hundreds of thousands of years, the force of gravity pulls hydrogen atoms together into a huge ball. *If* the ball is big enough, *then* there will be enough gravity pulling inward to cause the hydrogen atoms to change. That is, their nuclei become fused together at high temperatures to form a heavier nucleus of helium while ejecting high-speed neutrons. The newly formed helium atom now weighs slightly less because of the process of fusion. Part of the mass of the two hydrogen atoms has been converted into energy (i.e., radiation and heat) that we see burning in the sky. As human beings, we have adapted to various climates and have developed the capacity to manipulate signs, symbols, and concepts in order to provide ourselves with highly practical means for understanding ourselves, our environment, and surviving on this planet.

From the examples of artificially generated energy and natural energy above, we can clearly see how scientific subjects can be separated into two distinct areas:

1. Those dealing with purely academic or intellectual concerns (our theoretical knowledge of the physical universe)
2. Those dealing with more practical concerns (the invention, development, and use of technology)

In the first area, the topics can range from knowledge of the structure of the universe and the underlying components of matter to the theory of evolution, and so on. In the second area, the topics deal more with what affects us every day (e.g., will that bridge support our weight? or what medicines will help cure cancer?).

Further examples of academic or intellectual concerns include the expansion of the universe, the big bang and the steady-state theories, and theories of the continuous expansion and contraction (or oscillating) of the universe. Astrophysicists have hypothesized that if the matter in the universe is less than one atom per eighty-eight gallons of space, the universe will continue to expand or will reach a steady state. If the matter is greater than one atom per eighty-eight gallons of space, the gravitational attraction between these particles will be great enough to cause the universe to slowly contract and inevitably collapse in on itself. Such a theory has very little practical concern to us because we will not be around at such a time. The sun keeps shining, and life goes on. However, it does present information on a very grand and thought-provoking level. That is, it gives us reason to think about ourselves and our place in this universe in a much more profound way.

Examples of practical concerns include climate change, cigarette smoking or vaping (and the connection between lung cancer and coronary heart disease), cloning, and genetically modified organisms.

WHY STUDY SCIENTIFIC REASONING?

Studying scientific reasoning will keep us better equipped to understand and evaluate scientific information, thereby making us better critical thinkers. Society has become increasingly more complex and diversified, and in order to filter through and make sense of information, we need some way to understand it. In addition, it is not just a coincidence that scientific reasoning has become the most popular form of attaining knowledge concerning the cause-and-effect relationships of the physical world. It is characterized by an element of universality and objectivity, it has a very good track record of success in predicting novelty, and it provides the greatest explanatory power of all our current methods of knowledge. For these reasons and more, science is the best method for attaining knowledge we humans have developed so far.

THE TRICKLE-DOWN EFFECT OF SCIENTIFIC INFORMATION

Science gets done in fieldwork, through studies, and in the laboratory. This information is then considered throughout a particular scientific community and disseminated in professional journals, conferences, and so on. These results may then get picked up by more mainstream popular journals, such as *Scientific American* or *Discovery*. Some results may then make their way to more popular magazines, such as *Newsweek* and *Time*, and then to newspapers, such as the *New York Times* and *USA Today*. Some will appear on shows such as CNN's *Science Week* and *NOVA* and on the Discovery Channel and TLC. Eventually, the results will make their way into the textbooks of universities, colleges, and high schools.

Do we need to be scientists in order to understand scientific reasoning?

Consider some analogies. Do art critics need to be artists themselves (i.e., musicians, artists, dancers, or actors)? Is it necessary for us to have played football in order to appreciate and understand the National Football League? Would it be necessary for a sports analyst to have played the game? One of the greatest sportscasters of all time—Howard Cosell—wrote a book titled *Never Played the Game*, which implicitly answers this question, yet he was one of the world's most respected authorities on both football and boxing. It is often the case that persons not trained in specific fields can bring unique insight to them by understanding related aspects that professionals rarely get a chance to see. Most of us will be outsiders looking in at what science is up to. We have already acquired some of the tools we will need in the analysis of scientific findings. We just need to learn a few more.

CAUSALITY AND CORRELATION

A *correlation* is a statistical relationship between any pair of things, groups, characteristics, qualities, and so on. Although every causal relationship implies a correlation between two variables, A and B, a correlation does not by itself guarantee a causal relationship. Correlations may be attributable to other factors, such as coincidence, chance or luck, or even another cause C not yet considered. As you are reading this sentence, you can count the number of letter c's to equal the number of seasons there are in a year. We could say that the four c's in the previous sentence and the four seasons of the year are co-related. But this is purely coincidental and a far cry from saying that there is any causal relationship between the two. We can see correlations between all sorts of things—it's easy if you try. Spotting correlations shows how well our minds are equipped to constantly identify comparisons—similarities and differences. Correlations are divided into three types:

1. *Positive correlation*—When observing two things, if a feature occurs with greater frequency in Group A than in Group B, it is positively correlated with the first group; for example, grade-school students who take piano lessons (Group A) tend to do better in mathematics than those who do not take piano lessons (Group B). There is a positive correlation between piano lessons and proficiency in mathematics.
2. *Negative correlation*—When observing two things A and B, if a feature occurs with lesser frequency, the correlation is negative; for example, grade-school students who do well in math tend to watch less television than those who do poorly in math. There is a negative correlation between not watching television and proficiency in math.
3. *Neutral correlation*—When observing two things A and B, there is no correlation if there is no difference between the level of B's in either A's or non-A's; for example, if IQ tests show no discernible difference between scores of blue-eyed people and brown-eyed people, then there is no correlation between IQ scores and eye color.

A wonderful website created by Tyler Vigen[3] shows how seemingly unrelated events or activities can demonstrate correlations. For example, there is a strong correlation between the amount of money the United States spends on science, space, and technology and suicides by hanging, strangulation, and suffocation. Also, you can find correlations between the number of people who have drowned by falling into a pool and films that Nicholas Cage has appeared in. Figure 5.2 shows a few more that demonstrate the latitude with which correlations can be made.

It would take quite a bit of work and a very good imagination to consider how the age of Miss America could be even remotely connected to how many people were murdered by steam, hot vapors, or objects over the course of a ten-year period.

Figure 5.3 shows another example.

Nicholas Cage has appeared in quite a few films over the course of this ten-year period—twenty-five to be exact. To think that his work had anything to do with the relative number of drownings by falling into a pool would be a bit of a stretch. Perhaps there's a movie to be made starring him regarding this very conspiracy. Probably not.

So we must be careful when citing correlations because they can be made between practically any two disparate things. Just as anecdotal experiences do not necessarily imply sound causal reasoning, if there are enough of them—as we saw with cardiac patients reporting on the side effects of Viagra—then we can establish a causal connection.

To understand *causality* is to consider the relationship between events. As we grow from childhood, we make associations about the world (e.g., injury–pain, rain–wet, and fire–hot), and then act accordingly. In science, there are two types of causes:

1. *Constant, or necessary, condition*—This condition is necessary for an event to occur; for example, oxygen is necessary for combustion. But we would not say that oxygen *causes* combustion. It is simply one of the factors necessary for combustion to take place. We know that *if* combustion is occurring, *then* oxygen must necessarily be present.

2. *Variable, or sufficient, condition*—This is the condition that brings about the effect; for example, although combustible material (dry leaves) and oxygen are necessary conditions for fire, it was the careless tossing of a lit cigarette thrown from a car

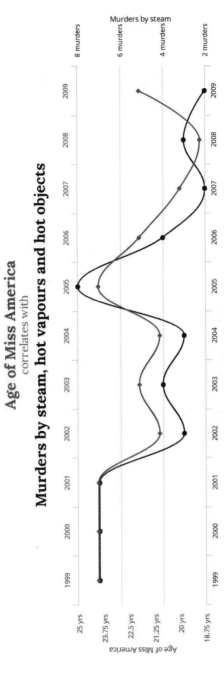

Figure 5.2

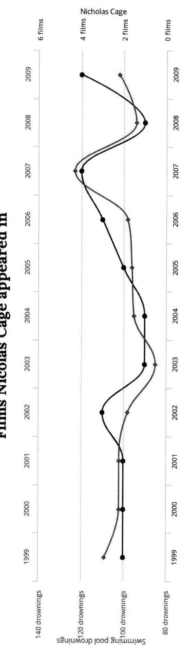
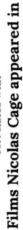

Number of people who drowned by falling into a pool
correlates with
Films Nicolas Cage appeared in

Nicholas Cage

Swimming pool drownings

● Nicholas Cage ◆ Swimming pool drownings

Figure 5.3

that started the forest fire. Dry leaves combined with oxygen do not suddenly catch fire. There must be some further cause that, when combined with the others, is sufficient to bring about this effect.

The set of both constant and variable conditions is the combined, or total, cause. In order to move beyond a simple correlation and attempt to establish a *causal* relationship between two things A and B, scientists sometimes use what are called *controls*. A control is a type of experiment in which scientists can regulate and monitor the subjects they are studying. In other words, they are trying to "control" the set of circumstances under which a suspected cause occurs. To do this, scientists again rely on that wonderfully comparative aspect of the human mind and separate at least two groups of things, subjects, animals, and so on under observation. This can occur in either a laboratory setting or a natural setting. The two groups are called, appropriately, the test (or experimental) group and the control group.

As we saw earlier, nondeductive forms or reasoning take place in the form of inductive generalizations and statistical syllogisms. That is, scientists must take the necessary means to ensure that the groups they are studying are well representative of the overall group for which this information will apply. The procedure itself is relatively simple. That is, the test group is given the necessary causal element in order to determine possible effects, while the control group is not given the causal element, so a comparison of the outcomes of the two groups can be made. Sometimes analogical reasoning is incorporated into this type of causal experimentation with the use of laboratory animals. Animals of specific types are held to be analogous, or similar, to humans in certain respects, so instead of experimenting on humans, scientists sometimes use animals. They would still maintain the two distinct groups regardless of the type of subjects under study.[4]

When humans are used in studies involving control and test groups, researchers must be extremely careful in collecting and interpreting information. It is not uncommon for researchers to taint or fudge their findings because they anticipate or expect particular outcomes to occur. In addition, it can become quite easy for a subject to give information she thinks the researcher wants to hear (sometimes referred to as the Hawthorne effect). For this reason, researchers deliberately "blind" their experiments in order to reduce bias and increase objectivity. There are generally two ways in which to blind an experiment:

1. *Single-blind experiments*—In these experiments, the subjects are not aware of whether they are in the control group or the test group.
2. *Double-blind experiments*—In these experiments, neither the researchers nor the subjects are aware of who are in the control group and who are in the test group. Only the person heading the study knows who is in which group.

A good deal of drug testing in medical research is double-blinded. Those in the test group are given a new experimental drug, while those in the control group are given a *placebo* (or sugar pill, i.e., a pill that has no effect on the subject). Not until all testing is completed do the researchers know who were in which group. The blinding of experiments is an extremely creative way in which enforced ignorance of specific factors leads to greater objectivity.

THE SCIENTIFIC METHOD

Scientific evidence is often obtained by using what has come to be known as the *scientific method*. Although there is much debate surrounding what the scientific method actually is, it can generally be described in the following steps:

1. We initially *observe* a phenomenon of some form.
2. We then make educated guesses, called *hypotheses*, as to why this phenomenon occurred.
3. We then make *predictions* as to the type of data we should expect to find if our hypothesis is correct.
4. We then proceed to conduct experiments and gather *data*.
5. We are then faced with three possible outcomes: the gathered data support our prediction and *confirm* our hypothesis, the gathered data fail to support our prediction and *falsify* our

hypothesis, or there is not enough data to determine one way or the other.

6. Finally, we need to consider if there are any *other competing hypotheses*.

Figure 5.4

Here's an example of how we might use the scientific method. Let's say you were sitting at home and a large branch from a tree crashed through the roof of a house nearby:

1. This is the first step of the scientific method. Your initial *observation* of a phenomenon is that a large tree branch crashed through the roof of a house.
2. In step 2, you would consider why this occurred, and in so doing, you would come up with any number of educated guesses, or *hypotheses*, as to why this happened. For example, it could have been due to a lightning strike. It could have been due to vandalism. It could have been the result of animals living in

the tree. It could have been due to termites eating away at the tree. It could have been due to the age of the tree. Or it could have been none of these and was due to a cause we have yet to consider.

3. In step 3, you would make *predictions* about what type of data you would expect to find if one of your hypotheses were correct. If the cause of the fallen tree limb were due to lightning, you would expect to see signs indicating that this was the case. If there was no storm activity that day, this can quickly be ruled out and falsified. If it were due to vandalism, you would expect to find signs of this type of activity, such as signs of sawing or tampering with the tree limb. If the cause were due to animals living in the tree, you would again expect to see signs of this type of activity, such as woodpeckers, squirrels, or raccoons. If it were termites, this would easily be detectable by noticing their hollowed-out columns within the tree itself, especially around the point at which the branch broke. Finally, if it were due to age, this would be evident in the physical state of the branch and the tree itself.

4. In step 4, you would then proceed to investigate and collect *data* based on your proposed hypotheses and predictions. In other words, you would be looking for clues like a detective.

5. After collecting data, you will move on to step 5 and find that your data support your prediction and *confirm* one of your hypotheses, that the data fail to support your prediction and *falsify* your hypothesis, or that you have not found enough data to determine why the tree branch fell onto the roof.

6. Remember that you cannot forget step 6, which reminds us that there may be an *alternate hypothesis* that could explain the cause of the phenomenon. Even if we have attained enough data to support our prediction and confirm a hypothesis, we must always consider other factors that may provide further support as an explanation.

It might also be necessary to appeal to various experts in such situations. In terms of experience and authority, people familiar with the structure of trees, such as arborists, might be brought in as experts to make such a determination. Large tree branches falling on houses is something we need to take very seriously, and we want to be assured that this type of event can be prevented in the future. So we would be well advised to appeal to the authority of such an expert, who is far more familiar with trees than the average person, to make such determinations.

At this point, it is important to remember that this example is an ideal situation used to demonstrate the power of the scientific method. But as critical thinkers, you should know that the process of science is much messier than this and far more politically complex. Many of the topics within both the natural and the social sciences are extremely complex, and trying to understand the causal factors behind those complex aspects of nature is extremely difficult. In addition, in the past forty years or so, far less attention has been paid to replicating the results of specific experiments. Many studies within various scientific communities go unchallenged and uncorroborated, and this is irresponsible. One meta-study in *Nature* magazine looked at one hundred psychological studies and tried to replicate the findings of each study but could only do so with only thirty-nine of them.[5] This gives us some indication of the way in which the scientific community at large has changed in holding itself accountable for process and discovery through the peer review process.

In addition, you should also know that the entire political process of science has evolved to the point that it is very important for institutional scientists at universities to be successful so that they can continue to receive grants that can bolster the reputation of the university that hired them to get them the money to become successful in order to bolster their reputation and so on. Perhaps Richard Smith, former editor of the *British Medical Journal*, said it best when he claimed that most scientific studies are wrong and that they are wrong because scientists are interested in funding and careers rather than truth.[6]

Far too little attention is now paid to the scientific studies that did not work and the failed discoveries that were never recorded. So much emphasis has been placed on success in confirming hypotheses in science that little attention is being paid to the falsified hypotheses. As a result, this has created an unnecessary imbalance that has been perpetuated for decades to praise and honor only the successes. There was a time when scientific failures had far greater value because they allowed the scientific community to know what avenues *not* to pursue in terms of scientific investigation. Such failed studies are valuable because they can save a lot of time, energy, and money. Some efforts are being made to establish databases of failed scientific theories and studies so that researchers can better understand what works and what does not work in the development of scientific hypotheses by encouraging researchers to share and publish their negative results.[7] If scientists are to be good critical thinkers, they need to know better the context in which they are conducting their investigations. That means they all need to have access to all of the results of all of the studies, not just the successful ones. So don't think that science is pure and smooth in its operations; it isn't. It's quite messy on a number of levels. The important point to note here is that, in terms of evidence, even with all its faults, it is still the best method for understanding cause-and-effect relationships in the natural world.

Consider another example. Let's say you're in a building somewhere and you hear a tremendous crash. A bunch of people have gathered around and discover that a stairwell in the building has crashed to the floor. Nobody was hurt, but all of the stairs have collapsed. So that's step 1: we observed a phenomenon—namely, the stairs have collapsed. In step 2, we consider what might have caused this to happen. There are a number of possible causes. Maybe there was an earthquake that was not detected and did not affect any other part of the building but the stairs. Maybe the stairs were improperly built: engineering codes had been violated, and workers cut corners to save money. Perhaps it was simply wear and tear. The stairs might have been very old and were decaying, and it just took time and wear and tear to cause them to collapse. Perhaps it was an act of vandalism. Perhaps somebody tampered with the stairs in a way that caused them to crash. We have presented four possible reasons (or conclusions) as to why the stairs might have collapsed. So who's right? With each educated guess or hypothesis, we have to make predictions. If it was an earthquake, then we predict that we should see signs that there was an earthquake. We could contact geologists at a nearby seismic reading station to determine if there was such an event on that day and at that time. If it was a case of wear and tear, then we should see signs of that in the debris. If it was poor building construction, then we should make determinations that this was the case. Finally, if it was vandalism, we should see obvious signs of human interference and deliberate activity. Now, in step 4, we roll up our sleeves and sift through the rubble of the stairs to try to determine what data exist. If we do make determinations that demonstrate confirmation that the data do positively support one of our predictions, then we have confirmation of our hypothesis. For example, if engineers can discover that the rebar in the cement construction had aged or was not used properly, it might be the fact that poor workmanship was responsible for it. You can see why this is important. We want to know who was responsible and potentially libel for such an accident. If people could have been harmed, we want to make sure that this never happens again. But this is how we do science every day. Every day of our lives, causes occur, and we witness the effects and want to know why those causes occurred so that we can better understand and accurately predict this type of behavior in the future.

SCIENTIFIC STUDIES

The second part of scientific evidence we need to consider involves scientific studies. Such studies often rely on statistics. As Mark Twain once said, "There are three types of lies: lies, damned lies, and statistics." As I've often maintained, 67.52 percent of all statistics are made up on the spot. So if you're going to try to talk nonsense to someone, be precise. As we have seen with elections in the past, the results of polls and statistics can be accurate or misleading. The majority of information is dependent on how the polls or studies were conducted and how the information from them has been interpreted. If you decide to quote studies or polls as evidence to support your premises, you need to consider a number of factors. Whenever anyone tries to use their findings as support for their premises, you can become empowered by asking the right types of questions, and when you know what those questions are, you are much more capable of better sifting through the type of evidence that people are using in support of their premises to maintain a particular conclusion. Here are the most important questions anybody should consider about scientific studies:

1. Who conducted the scientific study?
2. What was the motivation for the study? In other words, why was a study conducted in the first place?

3. Was the study funded? If so, by whom?
4. What was the methodology of the study? How was the study carried out? In other words, was the sample size of the study a good representation of those under consideration? Were there enough people or subjects involved in the study to maintain that it was a fair representation of the group being studied?
5. Is the study repeatable? Would any scientist under similar conditions conducting the same study arrive at the same conclusions?

I remember listening to our national radio station (CBC Radio 1) one evening and heard a news story about a study that was conducted regarding what was better: drying your hands with paper towels in a public washroom or drying your hands with an air-blown dryer. The point of the study was to demonstrate that air-blown hand dryers do not sufficiently dry human hands. As a result, moisture is left on the hands, which then touch the door handle and other objects, allowing bacteria to survive on hard surfaces longer than if hands were dried with paper towels. When I first heard this, it made sense to me. When you think about it, air-blown hand dryers often don't sufficiently dry hands because people don't leave their hands under them long enough. Men most often end up wiping them on their pants. I'm not sure what women do. Anyhow, the next night, I was listening to the same radio program and found out that after a bit of investigation, it turned out that the study had a very small sample size of a very few washrooms and a very few number of people coming out of those washrooms. It was then discovered that the study was funded by the paper towel industry of Canada. So this leaves us to believe that it might not have been the most fairly conducted study. So the conclusion—that is, that paper towels are better than air-blown dryers—might not be fully justified.

Another example of a flawed scientific study was carried out at the University of Arizona in 2006. In this study, Dr. Charles Gerba compared various occupations in order to see which one was the most "germy." His findings concluded that among most professions, teachers and accountants were exposed to the most germs because of their proximity to keyboards, phones, mouse pads, and so on. At first sight, there is nothing overly suspicious about Dr. Gerber's findings. However, when we start to ask some of the five questions above, we find that his research was funded by the Clorox Company. This now leads us to consider what the motivation for the study might have been. The so-called article listing the findings of the study turned out to be a press release sanctioned by Clorox. And at the very end of the article, a paragraph is devoted to informing us about the magnificent properties of Clorox disinfecting wipes. So what appears to be a scientifically motivated study is actually a promotional device used to market and sell a cleaning product. Known as "native advertising," this hybridized form of pseudo-news and marketing copy has generated new challenges for consumers to consider. One would hope that the industry is guided by ethical principles of transparency by specifically stating that such infomercials are deliberate forms of native advertising. Otherwise, the viewer/consumer lacks the context of the advertisement.[8] When stated in the guise of a scientific study, it lends a level of questionable conduct to the argument and leaves us wondering about the trustworthiness of the findings.

There are many examples of various studies that fail to respond to these questions objectively and therefore are guilty of vested interest or commercial bias. When we ask questions like the five above, we become immediately empowered with the ability to challenge those who refer to such studies and statistics as evidence in support of their premises for any given argument. So if anyone uses a line like "Studies show that . . ." in an attempt to support their argument, you have the right to ask them any or all of the above five questions. Likewise, they have the right to do the same to you should you make a similar appeal.

Keep in mind, however, that scientific studies, when carried out carefully and properly, are still the best means available to us in trying to understand cause-and-effect relationships in the natural world. We should by no means throw the baby out with the bathwater here. But we must always be careful in considering evidence of any type—including scientific evidence—and always be on our guard against the deliberate manipulation of such studies due to vested interest.

THREE PHASES OF RESEARCH ON DRUG THERAPIES

One of the best ways to understand the importance of clinical studies is to consider the steps involved in the research of the effectiveness of drugs for specific therapies. All of us will, at some point in our lives, take medications for some type of ailment. But have you ever wondered how, exactly, those drugs came to be approved for human consumption? There are several phases for determining a drug's effectiveness, or *efficacy*, that must be carried out before the pills ever make it to our local pharmacy shelves:

> *Phase I*—First of all, studies are initially conducted to learn about the dosages required to produce a response in the human body and about how the human body processes the drug and to learn whether the drug produces toxic or harmful effects and at what dosages.
>
> *Phase II*—Second, a drug under consideration will be tested on a group of patients who have a specific disease. At this point, the drug is not a treatment per se but rather is the object of study to determine any benefits, side effects, and so on. If there are no benefits, the study stops. If there are benefits, researchers move on to phase III.
>
> *Phase III*—Finally, at this point, the intent of the drug experiment is to introduce a lasting beneficial change in the patients participating in the study with the intent to prevent or reverse the progression of the disease. There is a specific strategy involved of treatment experiments with patient participants at this stage. This leads us to the controlled clinical trial. It is important to understand this procedure because most people have no idea of how their medications have come to be proven effective.

THE CONTROLLED CLINICAL TRIAL

Clinical research on drugs or surgical treatments are undertaken in order to provide answers to specific questions such as these:

- Will this treatment prevent or remedy a particular disease?
- Will this treatment do more good than harm to patients with this particular disease?
- Will this treatment do more good than available alternative treatments?

The idea behind controlled clinical trials is to reduce bias in order to maintain objective, reliable observations. Dr. David Sackett (one of the world's founders of evidence-based medicine) and colleagues at McMaster University have identified at least thirty-five sources of bias that can distort the research process.[9] As we saw in chapter 2, if we are not careful, bias can skew our understanding, and in the case of medicine, it can do so to the point of rendering research useless and can create a false belief that ineffective or harmful treatments are therapeutic when, in fact, they are not. The purpose for establishing a clinical trial is to determine the effectiveness of a therapeutic treatment. The word *trial* indicates that there is a comparison between two or more potential outcomes. Sometimes the outcomes compared are null, or to consider the option of having no therapeutic treatment. At other times, trials may involve comparisons between current and newly developed treatments. In the case of the latter, the goal of the trial is to determine which treatment is superior to another in, say, safety or effectiveness. The word *controlled* refers to the comparative null set or group that receives no therapeutic treatment. It is often the case that a control group will receive a placebo rather than the actual treatment in order to compare the outcomes or effects of the study group. So there are often two groups that have a particular ailment. One group will be given a new therapeutic treatment, while the other group will be given a placebo. The most important aspect of such studies is that they are blinded. This is a creative and novel use of what we might call "enforced ignorance." Researchers deliberately single-blind or double-blind their experiments in order to maintain objectivity when compiling and later reading data. Controlled clinical trials in which the patients do not know what group they are in are known as single-blinded studies. However, when neither the patients nor the administrators of the test know which group they are in, the study is said to be double-blinded. The purpose of blinding a clinical trial is to limit bias on the part of the administrators. In other words, if neither the administrators of the test nor the subjects know who is in which group and who is receiving the new drug and who is receiving the placebo, this will ensure greater objectivity in determining the effectiveness of the treatment. Only the lead researcher knows who is in the control group and who is in the test group. By blinding the administrators and the subjects of the trial, the lead researcher can prevent bias on two levels: at the level of the participants and at the level of the administrators.

A few questions need to be asked concerning clinical trials: On whom do researchers study? How do they do this? How many subjects are involved?

Researchers use a technique called *randomization* in order to block selection bias. Patients are randomly assigned by a lottery system to receive one or another of the treatments under study. I have often wondered, however, to what extent these trials are strictly randomized. For example, if I am a wealthy industrialist and my son is dying of a particular disease, could I not "donate" a few million dollars to a new study with the assurance that he *will* be in the test group and therefore will be guaranteed of receiving the latest treatment?

Finally, the sample size of any trial must be sufficient in order to avoid chance occurrences; for example, it is possible to have a coin come up heads ten times out of twelve. But if you increase the sample, statistically, the ratio of heads to tails will even out proportionally according to the frequency of tosses. So, as with all studies, there must be fair and proportional representation of the group under consideration. It should be known, however, that such studies often fill up fairly quickly—especially with participants facing life-threatening diseases. Think about it: if you were dying of a disease and there was a new study with a potentially promising new treatment, wouldn't you want to be included?

For this reason, it has been suggested that clinical trials may be considered unethical because they sacrifice the good of individual patients for the good of society or the good of future patients. Be that as it may, many maintain that such trials are absolutely necessary if physicians wish to reduce the uncertainty of treatments. Physicians have an obligation to offer the best available treatment, and they cannot fulfill this obligation without conducting such trials.

To add a little historical perspective on such clinical trials, much of the research conducted on humans today grew out of the Nuremberg Code. This code emerged after trials following World War II on twenty doctors who had conducted medical experiments on humans that violated the laws of humanity. These experiments treated humans as objects or things as a means to an end, namely, further medical knowledge. Today, research on humans requires informed consent and, it is hoped, compassionate, conscientious, responsible researchers. The

Medical Research Council of Canada Guidelines provide a checklist of items about which patients must be informed.[10]

The universal foundational criteria of evidence have become benchmarks for determining what counts as acceptable and unacceptable in critical thinking. When we look at consistency, simplicity, reliability, relevance, and sufficiency, we can understand that evidence is extremely important and that we must be held accountable for the types of evidence we provide in support of our premises. So, remember, if you're going to use evidence in support of your premises, make sure you know what type it is and how well that evidence has been gained in reliable, sufficient, and relevant ways so that you have better support for your arguments. In other words, we all have a duty—an obligation—to follow where the facts and evidence lead us. When we ignore evidence and choose to "feel" our way through an issue rather than consider the relevant and reliably obtained facts, we have abandoned truth and meaning for what Stephen Colbert calls "truthiness."[11] Or, as Daniel Patrick Moynihan once said, "Everyone is entitled to their own opinion, but not their own facts."[12] Even though we have the right to believe anything we want, we must always be on guard to ensure that as critical thinkers, we seek out fact-based evidence to the best of our abilities. Otherwise, we may be guilty of committing errors in reasoning known as fallacies.

· 6 ·

Analysis of Fallacies

$\mathcal{A}t$ this point, we should have a pretty good idea of what an argument is and the types of reasoning we use on a day-to-day basis. We should also know how various biological and cultural biases influence how we interpret, consider, and act on information. In addition, we have understood why context is so important to interpreting information, and we have learned the practical application of diagramming arguments so that we can better understand their structure and represent and critique them more fairly. In chapter 5, we became more aware of the different types of evidence that can be used in supporting our arguments.

The final tool in the critical thinking skill set is to consider what aspects or elements might be wrong with an argument. These are called *fallacies*, and they all generally lead to the same result: inconsistencies and contradictions in human reasoning. Here's a personal example. When the movie *Star Wars: The Phantom Menace* came out, a fair amount of merchandise was spun off from its popularity. One piece of merchandise was a video game that we had purchased for our son. To play this game, two characters—Qui-Gon and Obi-Wan Kenobi— move about through various settings on specific quests, journeys, and missions, and the players get to control them. As our son was playing the game, I overheard Qui-Gon giving sage advice to Obi-Wan Kenobi in the following way: "Listen to and trust your feelings." But just a short while later, another piece of advice was being offered to Obi-Wan when Qui-Gon says to him, "Don't let your feelings cloud your judgment." Taken together, these two statements are contradictory. How would we know which feelings to listen to or trust, and how would we know which ones clouded our judgment? When both statements are taken together, they are inconsistent to the point of being contradictory. Either another premise must be added that informs Obi-Wan how to distinguish which feelings are to be trusted and which may cloud his judgment, or one of Qui-Gon's pieces of advice must be abandoned or ignored.

One of the quickest ways to spot inconsistency that we can clearly recognize is through hypocrisy. I know I have used Donald Trump as an example for several points throughout the book, and he has certainly had his share of inconsistent statements.[1] But let's consider some inconsistent statements of a past Democratic president: Bill Clinton. Let's recall when President Clinton said the now infamous line, "I did not have sexual relations with that woman, Miss Lewinsky." When he said this, he was lying. But he was not just lying; he was being hypocritical by virtue of contradiction. This is because Clinton was often seen touting "family and Christian values" to the public as his moral guide. As an apparent "good Christian," Clinton once stated,

> "I pray virtually every day." He asked Americans to pray that political leaders would remember Micah's admonition to "act justly and love mercy and walk humbly with our God."[2]

So how exactly does one claim to be a good Christian and yet have numerous affairs with various women out of wedlock and then lie about them? Perhaps Clinton simply figured he was a sinner and needed some forgiving. But the fact of the matter still stands: it was inconsistent and hypocritical for him to say this because, as we now know, he was indeed having sexual relations with Lewinsky and several other women as well.

In similar fashion, you might have also heard people say, "Do as I say and not as I do." This too is fallacious and inconsistent because it does not exonerate the person from what they're doing by telling others not to do it. So hypocrisy is usually the quickest and obvious example of inconsistency—although not the only one. But while we're on the subject, let's never forget: we are all hypocrites—every one of us. We just vary by degree and admission. Let's get back to fallacies.

A fallacy is an *error in reasoning*. There are two types of fallacies: formal and informal. Formal fallacies, as their name implies, deal with errors in their structure, or *form*, whereas informal fallacies deal more with the *content* of the arguments. We will consider the informal type of fallacies because they involve errors in reasoning that we commit every day, often without even realizing it. In this chapter, we will give specific names to some of the most common errors in reasoning.

Any online search will quickly reveal that there are literally hundreds of different types of informal fallacies. But for our purposes, we are going to consider only some of the most common in alphabetical order.

AD HOMINEM

The term *ad hominem* comes from the Latin for "against the man" or "against the person." One might also call it the *sticks-and-stones fallacy*. This fallacy occurs when we lose focus in our discussion and, instead of directing our attack against the content of an argument, focus on irrelevant qualities or characteristics of the person making the argument.

In other words, such a fallacy occurs when one focuses on the irrelevant qualities of a person rather than on what they are saying. One of the classic examples is this: why should we read anything by Oscar Wilde since it was clear that he was a homosexual? What does Wilde's sexuality have to do with what he wrote? So the statement commits the ad hominem fallacy and therefore does not make any sense because it is irrelevant and adds nothing to the dialogue of the value of Wilde's work. In addition, when President Trump calls various women "nasty," he focuses on irrelevant characteristics rather than dealing with the content of their arguments.

Although it is often tempting to refer to the characteristics of a person whom we find personally distasteful, these are never welcomed or warranted in a fair discussion or dialogue about important issues. In fact, an argument is almost immediately lost as soon as a person commits this fallacy. And if you thought that today's presidential debates are heated and filled with ad hominems (which they are), history reminds us that the principles of proper etiquette in disagreeing and getting along were somewhat abandoned in debates as far back as the Nixon era of the 1960s and 1970s. One of the most striking examples of abusive ad hominems in the history of American twentieth-century debate occurred between Gore Vidal and William F. Buckley Jr.

On the evening of Wednesday, August 28, 1968, at 9:39 p.m. on live television in Chicago at the Democratic National Convention, Gore Vidal—a left-wing, gay liberal—debated William F. Buckley Jr.—a right-wing, extremely not gay conservative. The two engaged in one of the most heated political debates of the time. The debate was live and moderated by ABC newsman Howard K. Smith. While discussing America's involvement in the Vietnam War and the rights of students to protest the war, the two men became engaged in an extremely heated discussion.

What followed was an emotionally charged series of ad hominem attacks, culminating in Buckley's threat to physically beat up Vidal. Here is a portion of their debate:

> Smith: Mr. Vidal, wasn't it a provocative act to try to raise the Vietcong flag in the park in the film we just saw? Wouldn't that invite—raising the Nazi flag during World War II would have had similar consequences.
>
> Vidal: You must realize what some of the political issues are here. There are many people in the United States who happen to believe that the United States policy is wrong in Vietnam, and the Vietcong are correct in wanting to organize their country in their own way politically. This happens to be pretty much the opinion of Western Europe and many other parts of the world. If it is a novelty in Chicago, that is too bad, but I assume that the point of the American democracy is you can express any point of view you want . . .
>
> Buckley: [interrupting] And some people were pro-Nazi.
>
> Vidal: [waving hand at Buckley] Shut up a minute.
>
> Buckley: No, I won't. Some people were pro-Nazi, and, and the answer is they were well-treated by people who ostracized them. And I'm for ostracizing people who egg on other people to shoot American Marines and American soldiers. I know you don't care . . .
>
> Vidal [loftily]: As far as I'm concerned, the only pro- or crypto-Nazi I can think of is yourself. Failing that . . .
>
> Smith: Let's, let's not call names . . .
>
> Buckley: [snarling, teeth bared] Now listen, you queer, stop calling me a crypto-Nazi or I'll sock you in your goddamn face, and you'll stay plastered . . .

[everybody talks at once, unintelligible]

SMITH: Gentlemen!

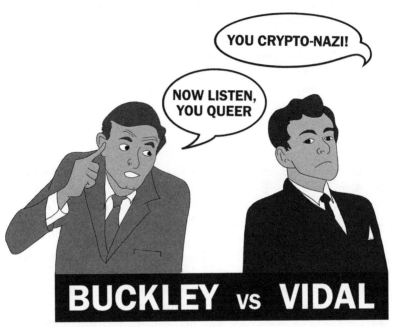

Figure 6.1. Buckley vs. Vidal

Buckley and Vidal were arguably two of America's most prominent public intellectuals at the time, yet both allowed their emotions and their personal attachments to their views to get the better of them. You can learn more about their tempestuous relationship in a documentary called *Best of Enemies*. We all know how difficult it is to maintain control during heated discussions. But as our critical thinking skills improve, in time we become better able to resist the temptation to let our more base feelings stand in the way of civil disagreement.

It is interesting how references to Nazis were used between Vidal and Buckley. In the past twenty years or so, it has become quite fashionable for political pundits and various members of the media—especially online—to use ad hominems in an effort to demonstrate the severity of their views. What we might call the *Nazi* or *Hitler* ad hominem occurs whenever anyone refers to another person's ideas or actions as similar to those of the Nazi military regime. Barack Obama's administration has been referred to as Nazi-like fascism. George W. Bush has been likened to Hitler. And now, of course, Trump. What's wrong with these types of references is that they tend to overexaggerate the seriousness of the situation while at the same time trivializing the devastating effects of the Holocaust and the millions who lost their lives during World War II.

An attorney in the United States named Mike Godwin has humorously developed a law that states that "as an online discussion grows longer, the probability of a comparison involving Nazis or Hitler approaches 'one.'"[3] So, if you've ever been involved in any kind of online discussions, you may have witnessed this firsthand. Godwin believes that the longer people discuss particular issues, the greater the likelihood that someone will use an ad hominem reference, comparing their ideas to those of Hitler or to Nazis. Known primarily as "Godwin's Law," it is sometimes referred to as "argumentum ad Nazium, reductio ad Hitlerum," or playing the "Hitler card."

It's not as though we should never compare the horrific actions of various dictators to those of Hitler. It's just that we need to avoid exaggerations and ad hominem attacks so flippantly while discussing important issues. Comedian Jon Stewart said it best: "You know who's like Hitler? Hitler!" So let's keep personal remarks to ourselves and focus on the content of the argument.

There are plenty of other examples of ad hominem attacks used by President Trump. Examples include Crazy Joe (Biden), Crooked Hillary (Clinton), Lyin' Ted (Cruz), Crazy Bernie (Sanders), Mr. Magoo (Jeff Sessions), Pocahontas (Elizabeth Warren), Cryin' Chuck (Schumer), Rocket Man (Kim Jong-Un), fake news (CNN, ABC, the *Washington Post*, and the *New York Times*), and enemy of the American people (mainstream media outlets). You may be old enough to remember the old saying, "Personal remarks are never in good taste." This is an old social custom or piece of advice that one would be wise to abide by in various settings. But ad hominem attacks or making comments on an individual's personal characteristics not only indicates that one is lacking in constructive, critical commentary but also demonstrates that one may be losing argument by resorting to such comments.

AD IGNORANTIAM

In English, this is referred to as the *argument to ignorance*, but it could also be called the *for all you know fallacy*. We are guilty of committing this fallacy whenever we make the claim that, *because* someone cannot find total and complete evidence for the truth of a claim, the claim must be false or, conversely, that since we cannot find total and complete evidence or proof for the falsity of a claim, it must be true.

If we believe that UFOs, ghosts, or psychic abilities exist because it has not been completely proven that they do not exist, we are fallaciously appealing to this kind of reasoning. You can literally use this type of fallacy to justify believing in the existence of just about anything. When children start to question the existence of things like Santa Claus, the Easter Bunny, and the Tooth Fairy, it is all too easy to say to them that their nonexistence has not been proven. Because of this, it means that they *must* exist.

For those of you who were told that supernatural beings like Santa Claus, the Easter Bunny, and the Tooth Fairy existed, do you remember when you learned that they were not real? What was that experience like? Were you upset by the fact that you had been duped all those years into believing that such important characters were not real? Was it a rite of passage from innocent ignorance to seasoned experience that you proudly possessed as a form of power over younger, more naive children who had not yet discovered the truth you had just learned? Or were you somewhat disillusioned that adults were able to perpetuate so many lies so easily and deliberately and kept you and all of your friends in the dark about them for so long? For many young children in the Western world, this so-called rite of passage was, in many ways, an awakening of knowledge from what William Blake called "innocence to experience." Did you ever think that if adults could lie about the existence of such characters, they might also be lying about other things as well? Did they really take your dog, Mr. Buttons, to a farm in the country so that he could run and play and be happy? Or did they simply have him put down and lied to you? Everybody would have their own unique experience of these so-called rites of passage. For some, they would be a form of enlightenment; for others, disillusionment and mistrust. It is interesting to consider to what extent we should propagate falsehoods to children today regardless of the perceived benefit during their time of accepting deliberate falsehoods.

Now that we have seemingly survived these epistemic rites of passage, we need to accept the fact that good critical thinkers must be vigilant in keeping the burden of proof resting squarely on those who make such claims. Simply because I do not know with 100 percent certainty that all UFO, ghost, and Bigfoot sightings are false does not necessarily mean that any of them are true. It is the responsibility of those who make such claims to provide the necessary evidence that will lead us to follow their argument to its logical conclusion. Since no such convincing evidence can be presented, we should not be led to believe that such things actually exist. To do so would be to fall into the trap of appealing to our ignorance. The most common practical example that avoids falling into this trap is in the regulated court system of civilized societies. Here, defendants are *presumed* innocent until proven guilty. Society would commit the fallacy of argumentum ad ignorantiam if they required the accused to prove their innocence. The burden of proof is kept squarely on the prosecution, who must demonstrate beyond reasonable doubt that the accused is guilty of the crime in question.

APPEAL TO AUTHORITY

Because we are limited in our knowledge about so many things, there are going to be many times throughout our daily lives when we must defer or concede to the authority of others. If I'm not feeling well, I see a doctor. I do not go to my mechanic. If I have car troubles, I do not go to my barber. So there are experts or authorities whom we must seek out in order to attain information, expertise, and the proper services. The appeal to authority becomes a fallacy only when we do so to a particular individual or group whose authority on the topic at hand is questionable.

"I was driving a Lincoln long before I got paid to drive a Lincoln," echoes Matthew McConaughey from earlier in the book. So we should purchase one too, right? McConaughey is a very good actor, but what do his acting abilities have to do with his authority in recommending good automobiles to purchase? The same holds true for any celebrity who endorses any product. Their fame and stature as recognized celebrities in no way makes them authorities on any particular topic. The authority I seek out for information regarding vaccinations comes from the World Health Organization, the Centers for Disease Control, and hundreds of peer-reviewed research papers from notable scientists, microbiologists, disease specialists, epidemiologists, and so on in order to better understand information about vaccinations, how they work, and their possible side effects. That's because, when it comes to factual knowledge and information about inoculation procedures, they are the best authorities. I do not seek out the authority of an actor who has virtually no understanding of how vaccinations actually function.

Keep in mind that an argument's strength stands on the solidity of its premises and how well those premises satisfy the universal foundational criteria, not simply on who endorses that argument. So proper appeals to authority are always secondary to the strength of the premises and the evidence provided in support of those premises.

AD POPULUM, OR APPEAL TO POPULARITY

This could also be called the *bandwagon fallacy*. You may have heard the phrase "jumping on the bandwagon." It comes from a reference used to designate somebody who only recently started agreeing with popular opinion. That opinion could be anything from the support of a local sports team that is doing well in the playoffs to a new idea or meme that is circulating around the Internet, the office, or the household. The main point of this fallacy is to demonstrate that there is no guarantee that the popularity of an idea is an indication of its truth. It was popular at one point in time to believe that the world was flat and that the sun revolved around the earth. But those days are gone—with the exception of Kyrie Irving of the National Basketball Association (NBA) and a few other NBA players.[4] At this point in the book, some readers might be thinking that we need to learn how to defend ourselves from so-called flat-earthers. Although there are plenty of sources that we can cite to demonstrate why it is more responsible and practical to believe that the earth is actually an oblate spheroid or geoid rather than flat,[5] there are times in critical thinking when we reach a point where it is no longer possible to fairly consider a counterargument. In the case of arguments stating that the earth is flat, there has been no compelling evidence to demonstrate that this is true. If there were, we would have to consider it as a viable alternative to our currently held understanding of the shape of the earth. So when it comes to subjects as bizarre as the shape of the earth, we must simply stop the discussion and move on with what we know to a far greater degree of probability. As with Bigfoot, the Loch Ness Monster, psychic phenomena, homeopathic remedies, astrology, crystal healing, traditional Chinese medicine, conversion therapy, ghost hunting, crop circles, levitation, psychokinesis, telepathy, Christian Science, Scientology, and many other pseudoscientific claims, should evidence be presented that is consistent, reliably obtained, relevant, and sufficient, we would be obligated to follow such evidence and believe such claims. Until then, we do not—and, more important, should not—believe such claims. Should any flat-earther produce evidence so convincing that we would have to believe it to be true, I would then change my current belief about the shape of the world. Until such a time, I have neither seen good reason nor witnessed convincing premises to believe otherwise. Now let's move on.

The days of believing that the earth is flat (and all other manner of pseudoscientific claims) are gone, largely because we have developed a better understanding of the way in which the natural world actually works. So the popularity of an idea in no way guarantees its truth. Proper reasoning, correct inferences, strong premises adhering to foundational criteria, and not committing fallacies or errors in reasoning are what strengthen an argument or an idea. At various times throughout history, people popularly justified slavery, forced prostitution, child labor, human battles to the death, and so on. Simply because they were popular and accepted at one point in time does not necessarily make them right.

There are, however, cases in which the popularity of ideas contributes to its justification. We find these in particular fields of scientific expertise. Within many of the sciences, there exists a level of professionalism in which peer members monitor the work of others and, over time, a consensus of understanding occurs in which specific ideas will receive a majority of approval. So there is a consensus of opinion within the natural sciences that accepts Einstein's theories of relativity, and this acceptance has gained considerably in popularity. But it is important to understand that Einstein's theories did not gain acceptance because they became popular; rather, they became popular because they were widely accepted by the scientific community and could be confirmed through the six steps of the scientific method that we saw in chapter 5.

As a collective of authorities within a given field, any appeal to strongly held ideas by a group of such people is not a fallacious appeal to popularity because the ideas to which they subscribe have gained in popularity *because* they have satisfied the criteria of scientific and logical rigor. Eventually, those with authority recognize such ideas and subscribe to them, and then they become popular within a particular group of authorities and throughout the nonscientific community. Of course, there have been numerous times throughout history when even the scientific community did not accept new and novel ideas about the natural world that turned out to be true, such as Semmelweis's germ theory, Wegener's theory of plate tectonics, and so on. However, the power of the scientific method eventually produced enough evidence to convince the scientific community that such theories were, in fact, true. It just took time and more and more evidence. But remember, as in the case with Einstein's theories of relativity, Wegener's theory of plate tectonics, and Semmelweis's germ theory, they did all of the hard work first, and *then* people began to subscribe to it. The theories stood on their own without the need for anyone's consent. The popularity of such theories came *after* scientists started to realize how relevant and accurate they were.

BEGGING THE QUESTION

This is the most misquoted fallacy in modern times. By definition, it is a fallacy that involves a form of *circular reasoning*. It occurs whenever any premise assumes the truth of the conclusion instead of supporting it. Consider the following examples:

> My psychic must have the gift of clairvoyance because only someone with clairvoyance could have known that I visited my grandmother in Brooklyn last summer.
>
> The reason why this car is so popular is because everybody wants one.

Even if the conclusions are true, the premises do not support the conclusions—they assume them. These arguments move in a circular fashion so that the conclusions support the premises, which in turn support the conclusions. The premises "beg the question" by assuming or stating the truth of the conclusion as support.

Consider another example: "Mary is a good dancer because she dances well" is a circular argument that begs the question of whether or not Mary actually dances well. Instead, the statement passes over Mary's talent by assuming the truth of the conclusion as though it is already established as a fact when it is not.

Everyone has their pet peeves. For me, it has been the wrongful use of the phrase "begs the question." For the past thirty years or so, the phrase has been used improperly by journalists, television talk show hosts, politicians, and the general public. It is difficult to determine who first began the misuse, but in the media, it has become fashionable to use it as a sort of "hip," newsy catchphrase. Consider the following improper use of the term by a news reporter:

> I'm currently standing outside of the collapsed building. The destruction is severe, and the casualty rates are high; it appears to have been built improperly, which begs the question, "How could this have happened?"

In this case, the reporter should have said that it *raises* the question, *poses* the question, or *suggests* or *invites* the question, but it definitely does not *beg* the question. The phrase "begs the question" is a fallacy specifically related to circular reasoning.

I still hear the phrase used incorrectly from time to time by journalists and news anchors. I came across an interesting website called *Beg the Question: Get It Right.*[6] The hosts of this site and its followers are attempting to bring attention to the proper use of this informal logical fallacy and to issue cards of notice to those who use it improperly.

So let's be careful when restating our premises so that our premises do not assume the very thing we are trying to support. Otherwise, we would be begging the question.

DISANALOGY

I sometimes refer to this fallacy as the *apples and oranges fallacy*. It is perfectly normal to make comparisons when we're trying to state a point, and when analogies are used properly, they can be extremely beneficial in helping people to understand a particular concept, an opinion, or a point of view. However, sometimes we don't always choose good analogies. When this is the case, we need to know why the comparison is not a good one. Here is an example of a particularly bad analogy: When Steve Coburn, co-owner of a horse named California Chrome spoke to journalists in 2014 about why his horse did not win the Preakness after having won the Kentucky Derby and the Belmont Stakes, he was visibly and verbally upset. He claimed that the winning horse, Totalist, beat Coburn's horse because it had not run in either the Kentucky Derby or the Belmont Stakes. Coburn's horse was aiming for the coveted Triple Crown of horse racing, but Coburn maintained that it's not "fair to the horses" to allow a horse that had not run in the previous two events to run in the third. The day after the event, Coburn stated what seems to be one of the worst sports analogies uttered in a good many years. In trying to make a comparison between allowing a horse into the third of a Triple Crown race when it had not competed in the prior two races, Coburn said this to a television journalist:

> You figure it out. You ask yourself, Would it be fair if I played basketball [against] a child in a wheelchair?

Aside from the fact that Coburn might be coming off as a bit of a sore loser, his use of analogy doesn't really make sense. How is entering a horse in a race (a horse that did not run in the two previous races of the Triple Crown) anything like an aged man playing a wheelchair-bound child in basketball? First, notice that Coburn has tried to make his point in the form of what's called a *rhetorical question*. A rhetorical question is not really a question at all; rather, it's a statement in the guise of a question. It is supposed to be so obvious a conclusion that we really don't need a response. It's like saying to someone, "Haven't we had enough of this rainy weather?" or "How about those Yankees?" We really don't want the person to respond other than to simply nod in agreement, that is, if it's been raining a lot or you're a fan of the New York Yankees. So Coburn states his analogy in the form of a rhetorical question that we cannot really agree to because he commits the fallacy of disanalogy. That is, his horse's loss to Totalist is nothing like him playing a wheelchair-bound child in basketball. Are we to believe that his horse is like the child in the wheelchair? If so, why? His horse and jockey were not harness racing. If he had to force his jockey to ride in a harness, Coburn's analogy would have been better, but, as it stands, it is a very bad analogy to the point of being disanalogous. For the record, depending on what child Coburn decided to play, there are some very talented wheelchair basketball athletes who might easily beat him on the hardwood, so his analogy fails on two levels.

Consider another example:

> Too many kids these days are consuming far too much soda. They are hooked on the stuff just like junkies are hooked on crystal meth.

The question we need to ask ourselves now is this: how similar and dissimilar is the consumption of soda to the use of a highly addictive drug such as crystal methamphetamine? If the two are far more dissimilar than they are similar, then one is guilty of committing the fallacy of disanalogy.

There are many analogies that have been used throughout history. One might say that most of literature involves analogies with extended metaphors, symbolic comparisons, and so on. From Shakespeare's lines "Shall I compare thee to a summer day?" to Forest Gump's statement "Life is like a box of chocolates," it would be very difficult for us to be able to navigate through this world without the use of comparisons with analogies. So, just as the crafty beaver carefully chooses which sticks to use in building its den, so must you be just as selective in choosing analogies to support your arguments.

EQUIVOCATION

The fallacy of equivocation is caused whenever someone uses a term, phrase, or sentence in an argument with two different meanings. Consider this example:

> (P1) Power corrupts.
> (P2) Knowledge is power.
> (C) Therefore, knowledge corrupts.

In the first premise, the use of the word *power* means political power and, hence, one's inherent weakness that possessing power will corrupt them to the point of abusing that position of power for personal gain. It's sort of like possessing a ring of invisibility. In the second premise, the word *power* refers to the ability of humans to be able to understand the natural world, and in so doing, we can become empowered to use that understanding to our betterment and the betterment of other species.

During any discussion, the fallacy of equivocation can arise if we engage in a verbal rather than a genuine dispute. With verbal disputes, we are guilty of each using a term differently. For example, if a grounds-keeper at a golf course told me he was going to kill all the gophers on the course and I thought he said "golfers,"[7] we would be dealing with two completely different issues. In order for there to be a genuine dispute, we must be referring to the same issue.

Consider another popular example:

P1: Nothing is better than eternal happiness.
P2: A half-eaten hot dog is better than nothing.
C1: A half-eaten hot dog is better than eternal happiness.

A popular example of the fallacious use of equivocation arises around the debates, conversations, and dialogues that people have about topics like creationism versus evolution. Some people will claim that evolutionary theory should not be taken very seriously because it is, after all, "just a theory." In this example, what people fail to realize is that they are equivocating on the word *theory*. They are not using the word in the same manner as evolutionary scientists use it (e.g., the theory of gravity, quantum theory, and so on), which comes from the Greek word *theoria*, meaning a natural explanation of some aspect of the world that has been strongly supported by evidence. Instead, they are using the word to mean less certain mental states, such as "hunch," "guess," or "conjecture." This is unfair. Part of the problem may come from a simple misunderstanding. While doing a quick, basic online search for the word *theory*, I found these two definitions directly beside each other:

1. A coherent group of general propositions used as principles of explanation for a class of phenomena: Einstein's theory of relativity. Synonyms: *principle*, *law*, *doctrine*.
2. A proposed explanation whose status is still conjectural in contrast to well-established propositions that are regarded as

reporting matters of actual fact. Synonyms: *idea, notion hypothesis, postulate.*[8]

Most of those within the scientific community will identify that the way
in which scientists use the word *theory* is that found in the first definition above, whereas those who tend to equivocate on the use of the term
evolutionary theory most often choose the second definition.

No matter which side of the debate we come down on, whether
dealing with the most mundane or the loftiest of topics, we must always be on our guard to make sure that we interpret terms, words, and
phrases in the manner that best represents their intentions. Otherwise,
we may be guilty of equivocation and of unfairly slowing the progress
of meaningful dialogue.

FALSE DILEMMA

This could also be called the *black or white fallacy* because it assumes
that there are only two choices, sides, or alternatives when in fact there
are more—perhaps fifty or more shades of gray. Whenever people state
that there are two and only two approaches to a particular topic, if you
can state a third, a fourth, or a fiftieth, then you have demonstrated how
that person has committed the fallacy of false dilemma.

You should also know, however, that there are genuine dilemmas.
Sometimes in life, there really are just two alternatives. Consider these
examples:

> Either time had a beginning or it did not.
> There's no such thing as being a little bit pregnant.
> When you die, your consciousness will either continue or it will
> not.

So a genuine dilemma does not admit to degrees between extremes.
But false dilemmas can be demonstrated by stating alternatives to the
proposed extremes:

> In my view, a person is basically entirely good or completely evil.
> Either you are a Democrat or you are a Republican.

To stop the massive number of concussions in American football games, we must ban the sport!

In each case, it should be noted that the speaker wrongly implies that the list of choices is complete. In the first case, a person's behavior could never be classified as being entirely good or entirely evil. All people are generally a mixture of different types of behaviors. But I know of no human being who has ever been entirely good or entirely evil. So I believe this statement to commit the fallacy of false dilemma.

In the second case, a person does not simply have to be either a Democrat or a Republican. Not only are there other candidates from other parties one could choose, but one can also be a right-leaning Democrat or left-leaning Republican. Thus, the category of *centrist* emerges. So there are quite a few other choices or shades of gray available in terms of political affiliations and loyalties.

Figure 6.2. False Dichotomy

In the final case, it's not as though we don't think concussions are bad; it's just that we don't want players—and perhaps our kids—to continue to suffer. But is banning the sport the *only* solution? A third possibility might involve changing rules about head contact, specific types of violent tackling, and other forms of contact that are likely to generate concussive effects. So, to say that either the sport continues or it must be banned is to commit the fallacy of false dilemma.

When people present ideas that indicate that there are only two choices available, we need to be aware that they might not be genuine but instead be stating false dilemmas. It is easy to assume that various aspects of the world can be neatly polarized in this way. It may also give the false impression that the speaker has done some research, that is, that after careful consideration, it appears that there are *only* two alternatives: A or B. Be wary of this when doctors tell you that there are only two possible outcomes available: the treatment they suggest or the harmful effects of the ailment. You should know that there is often more than just one treatment for any given ailment, and sometimes you need to ask for a second opinion to determine which treatment might be best for you.

HASTY GENERALIZATION

I sometimes refer to this as the *jumping to conclusions fallacy*. This fallacy is committed when one reaches a conclusion without sufficient premises. So this fallacy occurs when the foundational criterion of sufficiency is not satisfied by the premises. This error in reasoning is most clearly seen when people make generalizations from an insufficient number of particular events. For example, discrimination on many levels is often the result of hastily concluding generalized or broad conclusions that unfairly treat all members of a group the same due to the behavior of a few. Just as it would be a hasty generalization to believe that, with the occurrences of racial tension in the United States, all young black men are potential thugs and criminals, so equally would one commit the fallacy of a hasty generalization in believing that all police officers are racially biased and motivated. The root causes of hasty generalizations are often found in fear, ignorance, prejudice, and other biological and cultural biases, which can often lead us to make rash judgments. Hasty generalizations are drawn because we have been convinced of a conclusion before a sufficient amount of evidence or premises have been gathered.

The danger of making hasty generalizations becomes painfully clear in other areas as well, such as the field of medicine. Past historical accounts show clearly why it is important to gather a sufficient amount of premises before reaching a conclusion. The drug thalidomide (commonly distributed as Immunoprin, Distaval, and Contergan) was used worldwide during the 1950s and 1960s to treat various ailments, such as mild insomnia, anxiety, and morning sickness in pregnant women. It worked. However, for expectant mothers, it caused severe deformations of the developing fetuses, and thousands of children were born with underdeveloped arms and legs. It took five years before an Australian gynecologist, William McBride, made the connection between thalidomide and the effects of deformed limbs and babies. This discovery led not only to hundreds of lawsuits but also to the introduction of tougher regulations for testing, licensing, and reclassifying drugs.[9]

Meanwhile, in 1964, an Israeli physician named Jacob Sheskin was desperately trying to control the pain of many of his patients who were suffering from the skin lesions and boils caused by leprosy. Fearing that he had no other alternatives to minimize their pain, he administered doses of thalidomide so that they could at least sleep. To everyone's great surprise, by the next day, all of their skin lesions had disappeared.

Today, thalidomide is being used to treat specific types of cancers. In 1993, Judah Folkman pioneered work in the successful treatment of specific types of blood cancer, known as multiple myeloma, by administering thalidomide. Within six years, clinical trials and numerous journal articles demonstrated the efficacy of using thalidomide in treating multiple myeloma. By 2006, the Food and Drug Administration approved the use of thalidomide in combination with dexamethasone for cancer patients suffering from multiple myeloma.

Medical history has demonstrated that we must be careful in making hasty generalizations. In the initial use of thalidomide, the generalization was made that it was an excellent drug in the treatment of a number of ailments, including morning sickness in women. Then it was discovered that thalidomide contributed to thousands of deformed babies, so the generalization was made that it should not be used in the treatment of morning sickness. But such a generalization did not stop further consideration of the possible positive effects of such a drug. Thankfully, for thousands of patients suffering from leprosy and multiple myeloma, the generalization did not include them.

It is not always easy to know when enough evidence has been gathered in order to make a reasoned assessment of a claim. We must realize that evidence in some areas will be more sufficient than in others. But we still need to keep asking the important questions in order to avoid arriving at generalizations too hastily.

POST HOC FALLACY

The term *post hoc* is a Latin phrase meaning "after this." The full name of the fallacy is actually *post hoc ergo propter hoc*, which means "after this, therefore: because of this." Normally referred to as the post hoc fallacy, this occurs when someone assumes that because A precedes B, A *must* be the cause of B. Consider the following examples:

> Example 1: Every year during the National Hockey League playoffs, players often grow beards for good luck. When a team wins the Stanley Cup, many of the players have beards. It follows, then, that their growing beards caused them to win the Stanley Cup.

In this case, it is not the act of growing beards that causes the team to win the Stanley Cup. The team that happens to play the best and score the most goals will win the coveted Stanley Cup. There were plenty of other teams whose players grew beards, yet none of them won the Stanley Cup.

> Example 2: We should reactivate World War II air-raid sirens in our city to signal when tornadoes have been spotted in the area. Jonestown did this ten years ago, and they haven't seen a tornado since.

In this case, the person has mistakenly believed that because no tornadoes have occurred after the air-raid sirens were activated, it follows that the reactivation of the sirens must have been the cause of the decline in tornado activity. The actual reason for the lack of tornadoes may be due to coincidence, chance, or simply the lack of turbulent weather.

> Example 3: In an episode from *The Simpsons*, a wandering bear comes into the city of Springfield. The citizens establish a Bear Patrol to keep bears out of the city. Homer tells his daughter, Lisa, that since no bears have been seen, the Patrol Committee must be doing a good job. Lisa responds by saying that Homer's reasoning is specious. She says it is similar to saying that the rock she is holding is responsible for keeping tigers out of Springfield. By the same reasoning Homer used, she says that since no tigers have been seen, it must be due to the rock. Homer wants to purchase the rock.

What Homer fails to realize but Lisa clearly sees is that it is not necessarily the Patrol Committee that is keeping the bears out of Springfield. It is because there are simply no bears around—there was only the one isolated incident. So the cause of the lack of bears is not due to the Patrol Committee but rather to the fact that there simply are no more bears wandering into Springfield.

> Example 4: What is the likelihood of my being in a car accident wearing a clown suit when I drive on Highway 401? It's pretty close to zero. Therefore, whenever I drive on the 401, shouldn't I always wear a clown suit?[10]

If I were to drive on a major highway in a clown suit and did not get into a car accident, it would not be the clown suit that has kept me safe on my travels. It would be my abilities as a competent driver, fair weather, low traffic volume, luck, and so on.

In each case, we can see how prior occurrences are not the actual causes for the eventual effects. The post hoc fallacy is often committed using hasty generalizations and anecdotal evidence. One of the most famous examples of this fallacy involves the claims of model/actress Jenny McCarthy that specific childhood vaccines cause autism. McCarthy witnessed her son experiencing signs associated with autism *after* he was vaccinated, so she mistakenly believed that the order of the events pointed directly to the singular cause of her son's vaccination. Unfortunately, the premises of her argument were extremely weak and were unable to satisfy the foundational criteria of consistency, relevance,

Figure 6.3.   A Clownish Post Hoc

reliability, and sufficiency. In addition, there is very little scientific evidence supporting McCarthy's claim. It follows, then, that it would be more responsible to believe that the causes of her son's autism were due to other factors. If, at some point in the future, evidence can be produced demonstrating a causal connection between vaccinations and autism, then we would have to follow where that evidence leads us. However, this has not been the case. Regardless of the overwhelming amount of evidence for the safety and benefit of vaccinations, many parents in the United States have chosen not to have their children vaccinated. As a result, the incidence of diseases has risen and led to a considerable amount of sickness and discomfort and, in some cases, the deaths of children. According to the World Health Organization,

The United States has reported its highest measles case count in 25 years. In the WHO European region, there have been close to 90,000 cases reported for the first six months of this year: this exceeds those recorded for the whole of 2018 (84,462)—already the highest in this current decade.

The reasons for people not being vaccinated vary significantly between communities and countries including—lack of access to quality healthcare or vaccination services, conflict and displacement, misinformation about vaccines, or low awareness about the need to vaccinate. In a number of countries, measles is spreading among older children, youth and adults who have missed out on vaccination in the past.[11]

In learning how to think critically about important issues and how to disagree and get along, this is a very difficult topic to discuss because children's lives are at stake. But as with all matters in critical thinking, we must follow the facts wherever the evidence leads us. And the facts overwhelmingly support the benefits of vaccinations.

RED HERRING

This could also be called the *something smells fishy fallacy*. This fallacy occurs whenever one states a premise or premises that are not relevant to the conclusion and they intentionally try to distract our attention away from the topic at hand. In this way, one shifts the topic so that the focus is no longer on the originally stated issue.

To get a better understanding of what a red herring fallacy is, consider the following analogy. Imagine that a prisoner has escaped from jail and the guards are following him with bloodhounds that are picking up his scent as he runs through the forest. The prisoner knows that he will eventually be caught because his scent will lead the dogs right to his location. However, our clever prisoner has a large smelly fish with him that he borrowed from the cafeteria. He drags the fish behind him as he runs through the forest, and as the dogs come across the smell of the fish, they lose his scent, so the prisoner escapes. In the same manner, when people commit red herring fallacies, they're trying to throw us off of their scent, as it were, in the hopes that they can escape being held accountable for their beliefs or actions. Red herrings work very well in murder mysteries. We often suspect one character or another, and the plot development leads us to rethink who the actual murderer might be. Unfortunately, such tactics also work quite well for politicians.

Consider the following excellent example from an episode of *Family Guy* in which townspeople are asking mayoral candidates about specific policies:

> MORT GOLDMAN: Mayor West, if elected, would you increase the frequency of garbage pickup?
>
> MAYOR WEST: Well citizen, that's an excellent question, and I thank you for it. I think it's great we live in a town where you can ask questions. Because without questions, we just have answers. And an answer without a question is just a statement.
>
> MORT GOLDMAN: Oh, I like him. He looks me in the eye.[12]

It's clear that Mayor West's response has nothing to do with whether the frequency of garbage pickup will be increased. Mort Goldman has fallen for the charm of a candidate using a red herring, which has distracted him away from the topic at hand. In the political satire movie called *The Campaign*, comedian Zach Galifianakis referred to his political opponent's red herring response to a debate question as the "DC dip and twirl" maneuver.

Whatever name it happens to go by, the red herring fallacy is usually a deliberate attempt by a person or organization to avoid directly responding to a specific question. One of the most famous (and obvious) red herrings in the twentieth century took place during the murder trial of O.J. Simpson. Simpson's defense team, led by Johnny Cochrane, stated that Simpson was framed for multiple homicides because of collective racial hatred, at several levels of police and forensic investigation within the Los Angeles Police Department (LAPD). Cochrane was very successful at diverting the jury's attention away from the hard facts of the case and had them preoccupied with the incredibly unlikely possibility that Simpson was framed because of racial hatred.

In the case of the Simpson trial, the entire world was watching it on CNN for more than two years. There was an overwhelming amount of evidence implicating Simpson as the murderer of Nicole Brown Simpson and Ronald Goldman. However, at the time, the LAPD *was* involved in numerous beatings of black men—the most public being that of Rodney King. Millions of people, including myself, did not want to believe that Simpson could kill two people. However, the evidence suggested otherwise. All of the jurors should have followed where the evidence led them: to a verdict of guilty on both counts of murder. But some of the jurors were swept up by the brilliant defense tactics of Cochrane, who played the race card to the great benefit of his client, and in so doing, the entire world witnessed what was arguably the greatest red herring in the history of American justice. As entertaining as Simpson's trial was, we must never forget that two people were brutally murdered

Figure 6.4. If the glove doesn't fit, you must acquit

and that a man got away with a double homicide as the entire world watched some of the members of the jury ignore the most important evidence of the case and instead chose to follow an elaborate and very well-presented red herring.[13]

So be fair in your discussions and answer questions truthfully without the willful intent to mislead. If everyone avoided such tactics, we would all be better off.

THE SLIPPERY SLOPE FALLACY

Imagine you are standing at the top of a large hill. Now imagine that the hill is covered from top to bottom in ice. Now imagine that you want to travel only a short distance down the hill. However, as soon as you take your first step, you will not be able to stop. No matter how hard you try, you will not be able to climb back up the hill, and you will inevitably slide down it until you reach the bottom. The same idea holds true with the slippery slope fallacy. This fallacy occurs when people argue against the occurrence of a particular action because they believe that once started, it will inevitably lead to an unavoidably bad result.

So the slippery slope is a metaphor for a chain of causal events. Once a single cause starts, it will create an effect that will be the cause of another effect and so on until the final effect results in something rather undesirable. As a metaphor, the slippery slope describes the compounding effect or long-term consequences of our actions so that once we get started, we may not be able to stop. Many of us will have experienced either using or hearing someone use this form of reasoning at some point in our lives. There is the classic warning that smoking pot is simply a "gateway drug" that will invariably lead you to try uppers, downers, LSD, mushrooms, PCP, cocaine, heroin, and so on. These actions will lead you to become a drug addict, and you will be forced to prostitute yourself or steal from or rob people in order to support your habit; eventually, you will either end up in jail or die—all because of one shtick of the stuff.[14] To be fair, there have been people who have followed this exact path down their own slippery slopes. Sadly, Jim Morrison, Janis Joplin, Jimi Hendrix, and Kurt Cobain all experienced this unfortunate path. But this does not mean that every person who tries marijuana will inevitably slide down the slope and die. There are millions of people

Figure 6.5.   The Slippery Slope

who smoke pot and maintain fairly active, healthy lives without ever having moved on to harder drugs. Or perhaps they did harder drugs and now just smoke pot or now don't use any substances at all. Surely, the continued existence of Keith Richards must prove this. We can identify when a person is guilty of committing the slippery slope fallacy whenever we can demonstrate that simply by starting at the top of the slope does not necessarily mean that the series of adverse events will inevitably lead to the bottom of it.

One of the most common examples in recent history that references the slippery slope is the debate that exists regarding euthanasia (mercy killing or doctor-assisted death).[15] Allowing a person to make a decision regarding their end-of-life care is liberating for some people and quite distressing for others. This will be one of the topics we consider in the next chapter, but for now, our concern is with the manner in which the slippery slope metaphor has been used in popular dialogue recently. Those who do not favor assistance in dying often cite the possibility that allowing terminally ill patients the power to end their lives will generate more frequent use of this method for end-of-life care for less severe medical ailments. So today, we euthanize for stage IV terminal cancer; next year, we euthanize for people suffering from AIDS; the year after that, we euthanize for stroke; and so on until, little by little, we find ourselves euthanizing people simply because they were having a bad hair day. All joking aside, we need to take into consideration to what extent a slippery slope regarding euthanasia could become a reality and to establish responsible and experienced committees to ensure that a slide down such a slope does not occur in the future.

STRAW MAN FALLACY

I have often referred to this as the *caricature fallacy*. Again, fairness is the cornerstone of critical thinking. If we all play by the rules fairly, this may not guarantee that there will be less disagreement, but it will greatly increase the likelihood of being understood. If we misrepresent another person's argument, whether intentionally or not, and then address the misunderstanding of that argument, we create a false interpretation, or caricature, of the argument—something neither real nor intended.

As noted earlier in the book, the straw man metaphor has been used for decades. Its name references the straw men that were sometimes used for military training. The trainees are not attacking real men but, rather, constructed or fake men. The same holds for straw man arguments. If we misinterpret a person's argument—whether intentionally or not—and then proceed to critique it, this misinterpretation will invariably lead to an irrelevant commentary because we would be guilty of not faithfully representing the intention of the argument. We owe it to ourselves and to others to faithfully establish their intended position and support for it. This obligation is simply part of what it means to be fair in critical thinking.

Figure 6.6.   Strawman Fallacy

Committing straw man fallacies wastes considerable time, energy, and money. This is because everything that is said about a misrepresented argument has no relevance. For example, politicians all too easily take the intentions of their opponent's arguments and misconstrue them to create a caricature—a fake or unintended straw man argument. In our own lives, we must be vigilant in steelmanning or representing our opponent's arguments in their best possible light. To do otherwise would be unfair and something that—according to the Golden Rule of dialogue—we ourselves would not want. Therefore, we ought not to do this. When we avoid committing such fallacies, we will have grown and, most assuredly, made it to the final step to better thinking.

In this chapter, we have considered the most common fallacies that people commit every day. We should take considerable care to recognize such errors of reasoning not only in the views of others but especially in our own. By avoiding such fallacies, we can go a long way toward successful and meaningful dialogue.

By now, I hope it has become clear that there are better and worse ways to think about issues. We have considered some of the most essential tools in the critical thinking skill set to become better thinkers, and these will allow us to engage in fair and intelligent discussions. As we now turn our thoughts to consider specific controversial topics, we will see how these steps can help us in facilitating meaningful dialogue and establishing common ground in an effort to alleviate or soften disagreement.

II

APPLYING THE ABCS OF CRITICAL THINKING TO IMPORTANT ISSUES

· 7 ·

Tools for Having Intelligent Conversations and Getting Along

*Y*ou are now in possession of the most important tools in the critical thinking skill set. Using these tools will allow you to have intelligent conversations, disagree, but still be able to get along with others who don't happen to share your particular views on various issues. If you are already familiar with the way in which I teach or write about critical thinking, you will already know that if you can remember the first six letters of the English alphabet, they correspond with all of the tools covered in the critical thinking skill set. So to remember each tool, simply remember the first letter of each in alphabetical order: argument, bias, context, diagram, evidence, and fallacies.

Let's now use these skills in the consideration of seven controversial topics. In so doing, let us keep in mind that the cornerstone of critical thinking is *fairness*. In other words, we need to be mindful of *what* each other is saying and present it in the best possible light. In other words, we must faithfully steelman their argument. This is what was referred to as the *Golden Rule of dialogue*. Only after we have done so and others have done the same to our views can we begin to fairly apply the critical thinking tools in an effort to critique the premises of the argument. After you have indicated that you sufficiently understand the intent of the person with whom you are having a dialogue and have been able to demonstrate this by stating it back to them, you can proceed to discuss the value of their argument. There may be some aspects with which you agree and others with which you oppose. Determine first the positive aspects of the argument and any and all common points where you agree. Be sure to initially offer constructive criticism prior to destructive criticism.

People are going to disagree. That's just a part of our nature; in many ways, it defines who we are. But there are better and worse ways by which to disagree. It's not as though we need to come to a resolution on every point of disagreement. In fact, there are going to be many times when such a point will not be reached. In such cases, we must have the intellectual maturity to recognize and understand the causal factors responsible for such disagreement. By calling out, presenting, and establishing our differing biases as well as the context in which thinking through those biases takes place, we can better appreciate why there are disagreements about important issues in the first place. We should, as good critical thinkers, want to hear what other people think, especially when their views differ from our own, and we should extend to them the same courtesies that we would want extended to ourselves. In this way, we enter into the realm of intelligent conversation with our eyes open, and in a civil manner, we will be able to discuss any and all variations regarding important issues no matter how controversial they may be. Let's now consider some of these controversial issues.

DISCUSSING CONTROVERSIAL ISSUES

When I was a much younger man, my mother warned me about the dangers of discussing sensitive topics in diverse public settings. "Christopher," she would say, "when in mixed company, one should never discuss sex, religion, or politics."

However, as Bruce Springsteen once said, "But mama, that's where the fun is."[1]

We know there are "hot button," or controversial, issues that almost immediately lead to heated discussions. However, one of the reasons that these topics are so controversial is because they are so important to our everyday lives and we are very much emotionally attached to them. But that's why it is so important to be able to have meaningful dialogues about them and have the freedom by which to disagree but at the same time still be able to get along with one another.

We are going to briefly consider seven controversial topics: euthanasia, abortion, gun control, capital punishment, same-sex relationships, religion, and pseudoscience. For the first six topics, I will state the polar opposite viewpoints. You can then better situate yourself either at one end of or somewhere along the spectrum between these two extreme polarized viewpoints. We will then look at some common ground that exists between each point of disagreement in an effort to demonstrate how each side can continue to disagree and still get along. For the final topic, however, I'm going to simply critique various forms of pseudoscientific claims. The reason why I left this topic to the end is to demonstrate how to utilize the tools of the critical thinking skill set in a fair but critical and cogent manner.

EUTHANASIA: PHYSICIAN-ASSISTED DYING, OR MEDICAL ASSISTANCE IN DYING

The Extreme Polar Views

For euthanasia: We should allow all citizens during any point in their illness—regardless of the severity of their condition—the right to decide when and how they wish to be humanely put to death.

Against euthanasia: We should never allow any citizen under any circumstance to have their lives ended intentionally. We must do everything in our medical power to keep a person alive for as long as possible.

On which side of this debate do you tend to fall? Why? What would your argument look like? How carefully have you thought about this particular topic? If you believe that euthanasia should never be allowed no matter what the circumstances, what has led you to have this viewpoint? The same holds for those who believe that people should be allowed to have their lives ended through medical assistance. What we tend to find when discussing these issues is the level to which personal biases play a part in formulating our thoughts and acting on those beliefs. Some people base their disagreement with euthanasia on religious grounds. If that's the case, why might a person currently have a specific religious perspective that disallows them from accepting personal control over end-of-life care? For those who wish to allow people the capacity to control how they wish to die, what evidence or premises have they developed in support of this conclusion?

Some people in the United States have argued that in allowing for the opportunity to discuss end-of-life care, in considering the possibility of assisted euthanasia, there will be so-called death panels that will execute Grandma at the first sign of a cold. As we saw in chapter 6, this particular viewpoint commits the fallacy of the slippery slope. This viewpoint maintains that, over time, illnesses that are increasingly less terminal will be sufficient grounds to allow people to end their lives. So it may start with stage IV terminal cancer but over time will be used for less severe illnesses. The fear of the slippery slope with euthanasia is that, once it becomes legalized for people with terminal illnesses, eventually the laws will become more and more relaxed, and we will be inclined to euthanize people with non–life-threatening diseases or that many will simply give up their desire to live and rush to the hospitals to be "put down."

But where does the actual evidence lead us? So far, in the United States, physician aid in dying, or assisted suicide, is legal in California, Colorado, Oregon, Vermont, and Washington. In all these states, the reports indicate that terminally ill people considering such an option do not always choose euthanasia, even when it is legally accessible. In fact, in Oregon from 1998 to 2002, only 129 people opted for physician-assisted death. So it does not appear that a slippery slope effect for euthanasia is taking place in any of the states at the moment. Currently, these figures suggest that fears driven by a slippery slope mentality have not been warranted. Because dying is the most difficult thing any of us will have to face, not only do we need to be particularly sensitive to the needs and desires of various patients who are facing such a difficult decision, but we must also honor the decisions made by those whose biases differ from our own.

Common Ground

The main common ground between those who disagree about euthanasia is the value of human life. Those who oppose euthanasia believe in what might be called the sanctity of life. That is, life is so valuable that one ought not end it prematurely. There are often—though not always—religious biases that contribute to this particular view. These biases might maintain that we are not responsible for our own deaths. God is. As such, the decision to end our lives is not ours to make. On the other end of the spectrum, for those who support euthanasia, the value of life is so great that one does not see the need for continued suffering during the end-of-life stages. To continue dying in agony makes no sense. To maintain a level of dignity during the process of dying, by having the ability to control how and when one wishes to die, is considered to be of the greatest importance.

Perhaps the greatest common ground between the polarized views regarding euthanasia is *choice*. Can we agree, then, that liberty and the freedom to choose how it is we wish to die is the common ground on which we can disagree and get along? Would either side really wish to live in a society in which euthanasia was either disallowed entirely or enforced rigorously? For those who do not wish to have medical assistance during the dying process, their choice should be honored. But, equally so, would we not wish to extend the same privilege to those who wish for medical assistance in dying? So even though we may disagree about the issue of euthanasia, do we have the intellectual maturity to accept the value of liberty and choice in making such a difficult decision?

ABORTION

The Extreme Polar Views

Pro-life: Never allow an abortion, no matter what the circumstances, context, or stage of the pregnancy.

Pro-choice: Always allow an abortion to proceed if a pregnant woman chooses it at any point in her pregnancy.

This is a very emotionally charged topic that often strictly divides people. Everyone will have their reasons for why they think abortion should or should not be allowed to take place. How well have we thought about why it is that we believe what we do when discussing this particular topic? On which side of the debate do you tend to fall? Why? What would your argument look like? How carefully have you thought about this particular topic? If you believe that an abortion should never be allowed, no matter what the circumstances, what has led you to have this viewpoint? Conversely, if the decision of an abortion is nobody's business but that of the pregnant woman, what are your premises in support of this view?

At this point, I'm going to introduce some conceptual tools that will allow us to better understand where each of us falls in terms of discussing the issue of abortion. The first tool is called the *sorites paradox*. The word *sorites* is Latin for "heap." Imagine that I have bags and bags full of rice and that I intend to create a heap of rice before your eyes. But I am going to do so only by taking a pair of zircon-encrusted tweezers and building the heap one grain of rice at a time. As I continue to add grains of rice and the pile becomes larger and larger, eventually it will reach a size at which you will say that it is a heap. Because we all differ in our views regarding when, exactly, a heap becomes a heap, this demonstrates a shadowy gray area of ambiguity that I call the *umbra of becoming*. This conceptual tool allows us to better understand states of being as they transition from a state of nonbeing, to becoming, and then to actually *being*. For example, how many hairs on my head do I have to lose in order to be considered bald? How many pounds do I have to gain in order to become fat? When exactly is a person tall? Or short? Or young? Or old? So the sorites paradox provides us with a handy metaphor that can be applied to the discussion of the issue of abortion.

Here's how it works.

As we saw earlier in the book, when it comes to abortion, there are generally three schools of thought: the conservatives, the legalists, and the gradualists. Conservatives believe that life begins when sperm meets egg. After that point, one should not interfere or terminate the fetal process of growth. There are many premises in support of this particular belief. Some are religiously based, while others are purely secular. A legalist, on the other hand, believes that life begins after a fully developed baby exits the mother's birth canal or is removed by Cesarean section. At that point, it is considered alive and worthy of legal rights as a human being. To a legalist, the stage of development of the fetus is immaterial because the woman alone has total control of choice over its continued development or termination. Finally, the gradualist believes that life begins somewhere between the point of conception and birth. That is, for a gradualist, a fetus becomes gradually *more alive* from the point of conception to the point of birth. With the sorites paradox and the concept of the umbra of becoming, you can now better determine how you view the status of a fetus as it moves from a state of nonbeing to becoming to being considered alive and deserving of rights.

It should come as little surprise that there are problems with each perspective. To illustrate these, I will use what are called *thought experiments*. These are "what-if" scenarios that allow us to more critically consider our currently held beliefs by considering what are called *entailments*. The term *entailment* simply means that a conclusion must logically follow a given set of premises. Within each thought experiment, we shall better understand the entailments through the use of the sorites paradox and the umbra of becoming as they relate to each of the three perspectives on abortion.

For example, if you are a conservative and you believe that life begins at conception, then what this would entail is that, if someone were to stand in front of you holding a petri dish with a frozen sixty-four-celled embryo in one hand and a two-day-old infant in the other hand and said that one of those beings was going to die and they left the choice to you, the choice might not be clear. However, to be consistent in your belief that life begins at conception, you would have to do something similar to flipping a coin. If you chose to save the two-day-old infant, then perhaps you are not entirely a conservative because you are admitting to degrees of being. In this case, metaphorically, the two-day-old infant has far more grains of rice than a sixty-four-celled embryo.

If you are a legalist and you believe that life and rights begin after the child has exited the birth canal or by Cesarean section, then this logically entails that the mother retains the right to abort the child up to the point of delivery. In other words, if a few seconds prior to the delivery of the child the mother asked that the life of the yet-to-be-born infant be terminated, this would have to be allowed since, by definition, the legalist does not believe that the almost newborn has any rights until it has become separate from the mother. If this makes you feel somewhat uncomfortable, perhaps you are not entirely a legalist. You, too, would be admitting to degrees of being. In this case, according to the legalist's definition, only a few more grains of rice (another contraction or incision) would have metaphorically made the yet-to-be-born infant alive and worthy of receiving legal rights.

Finally, if you are a gradualist and you believe that life and the rights of a fetus begin somewhere between conception and birth, then this entails that you would know exactly when this takes place. However, this raises the problem of deciding what criteria should be used in making such a determination. Is it the body size of the fetus? A heartbeat? A complete and functioning nervous system? A fetus's reaction to pain? Developed consciousness? There are many criteria to consider, and who is to decide which of these criteria have been satisfied or should be satisfied? If you believe that the rights of an unborn fetus should be preserved when it has a fully formed body, with a complete nervous system, then would you approve of an abortion ten seconds (or ten grains of rice) prior to this occurrence? If not, then we need to think more seriously about gradualism.

The entailment of each one of these positions faces conceptual and practical difficulties. It is hoped that these difficulties have been made more clear through the use of the sorites paradox and the transitional phases of the umbra of becoming. However, by understanding the complexities and entailments of this issue with greater clarity and utilizing the critical thinking tools of the first six chapters, it can become easier to understand why disagreements occur in the first place.

Common Ground

As you can see, in every one of these positions—the conservative, the legalist, and the gradualist—the sorites paradox and the umbra of becoming demonstrate how difficult it is to make clear determinations regarding the status of the fetus. How many metaphorical grains of rice are necessary to create a heap? Or, in the case of abortion, how well have we thought through our particular positions? With such conceptual tools to aid us in better understanding the complexities in discussing these issues, we can go a long way toward understanding how and why we differ in our views about such important issues. Choosing to have an abortion is an extremely difficult decision to be made by any woman. Understanding one another's biases, as well as utilizing conceptual tools like the sorites paradox and the umbra of becoming, can help us to better understand why it is that we might disagree and how it is that we might agree in an effort to appreciate such differences of opinion.

Again, the common ground that each side values equally is liberty or freedom of choice. Some are free not to have an abortion, while others are free to do so. Would either side really want to live in a society where the freedom to choose was not available and women were either forced to have abortions or forced to carry out their pregnancies to full term? We may not agree with or like what the other side believes. However, both sides share common ground with regard to the value of choice and the freedom with which to make our own decisions unencumbered by unwanted political pressures.

GUN CONTROL

The Extreme Polar Views

> Pro-gun: Allow total freedom of weapons possession in the home, in one's vehicle, on a plane, on a train, with a goat, on a boat, on one's person, to be carried while loaded, anywhere and at any time.
> Anti-gun: Collect and destroy all guns and legislate strict laws that have stiff penalties to anyone owning or carrying such a weapon.

As I write these words, there will be yet another mass shooting somewhere in the United States. Where on the spectrum of this debate do you tend to fall? Why? What would your argument look like? How carefully have you thought about this particular topic? Guns are funny things. They can protect people, they can provide food and sustenance, or they can terrorize communities and even entire nations. A gun's function is simple: it is a handheld machine that can immobilize or kill at a distance. Some people love them, and just as many hate them. They take lives, and they save lives. So how are we to control them? Each country has its own laws regarding the possession and use of firearms. Canadian regulations, for example, are much stricter than those in many U.S. states. Regulations throughout the rest of the world vary from excessively strict to very lax. It would seem that we live in a world where there will always be guns. We cannot get the genie back into the bottle on this one. So we are torn between simultaneously wanting people to have the liberty and freedom to possess and use firearms in a responsible manner and living with the devastating effects that result when they are used improperly.

Common Ground

What appears to be the biggest and most common concern among both gun advocates and dissenters is the reduction of harm. Most people would agree that when guns are responsibly purchased, licensed, stored, and used, the issue of harm is minimized and we are all on the same common ground regarding rights, freedoms, and liberties. However, accidents happen, and when they happen with guns, people die. Many of those people are children. The Centers for Disease Control found that in the United States between 2007 and 2011, an average of sixty-two children a year under the age of fourteen were accidentally shot and killed. Many of the children were around the age of three and had found handguns (belonging to their parents) improperly secured or stored. The other deaths were by young teens who were playing with the guns, believing they were unloaded. Nobody wants to see children harmed or killed. But is this the price that has to be paid for personal liberty?

A similar case can be made for the accessibility to guns and suicide rates. Those battling mental health issues, such as depression, schizophrenia, and bipolar disorder, are often faced with the very bleak and hopeless feelings of despair, which they believe can be resolved only by suicide. In these very dark moments, access to handguns provides what appears to be the only solution. According to the Centers for Disease Control, in 2011 in the United States alone, there were 42,773 suicide deaths. Half of those suicides were caused by gun infliction. Suicide is the tenth-highest-ranked cause of death among all Americans.

Whether we disagree on gun policies or not, what we can all agree to is the common ground of reducing harm from gun violence. Let us think very carefully about what we believe in terms of gun control, for the rights and liberties and lives of others are at stake.

CAPITAL PUNISHMENT

The Extreme Polar Views

Pro–death penalty: There are specific crimes for which the death penalty is the only just penalty.

Anti–death penalty: No matter what the crime, no person should be put to death as a punishment.

On which side of this debate do you tend to fall? Why? What would your argument look like? How carefully have you thought about this particular topic? If you believe that capital punishment should never be allowed, no matter what the circumstances, what has led you to have this viewpoint? The same holds for those who believe that people should be executed for specific crimes. Do a bias check and consider the factors that have led you to believe what you now do.

There are several different motivations for punishment that sharply define and divide specific camps. In the first camp, there is the notion of retributive justice: the idea that the punishment should fit the crime. The retributive theory states that punishment should be equal to the harm done, either literally an eye for an eye or more figuratively, allowing for alternative forms of compensation. The retributive approach tends to be retaliatory and vengeance oriented.

Another approach is utilitarian, which maintains that punishment should increase the total amount of happiness in the community. This often involves punishment as a means of reforming criminals, incapacitating or incarcerating them so that they cannot repeat their crimes, and deterring others. For utilitarians, the purpose of punishment is to create a better society, not revenge. Punishment serves to deter others from committing crimes and to prevent the criminal from repeating his or her crime.

Then there is the restorative approach. This school of thought believes that there should be a variety of different types of punishments for different types of crimes but that the ultimate goal for punishment is to balance or restore the harms of the crime to the counter harms of the punishment.

Whichever camp you happen to belong to, it would be beneficial to consider why others might have a differing viewpoint. For those who believe that there are specific crimes worthy of capital punishment, what are those crimes? Should capital punishment be reserved for only the most heinous of crimes? Should specific contexts, acts involving murder, kidnapping, torture, rape, and so on be reserved for the death penalty?

For those who believe that capital punishment should never be an option regardless of the crimes, what are your premises for maintaining this viewpoint? How would you feel if your child was abducted, tortured, raped, and killed? Would you be able to control your baser instincts against the perpetrator for vengeance and harm? Would you be able to accept your own current convictions that no crime deserves the death penalty when someone you love so much has been treated so horrifically? Or would you want that person put to death for what they have done?

The most difficult aspect of critical thinking is to control our emotions and our passions through reason and fairness. But like the image of the charioteer trying to allow the "facts horse" to follow the path of evidence to truth while struggling to control the "biases horse" which is pulling away from the path, this is not always an easy thing to do. So we must remember the critical thinking tools of the first six chapters during the discussion of these extremely emotionally charged issues.

Common Ground

We may not all agree on if or when there should ever be a need for capital punishment. For example, those in favor of it will try to support their premises with statistics that demonstrate how such a punishment deters future crimes. Those against it will cite studies that demonstrate no connection between capital punishment and the deterrence of crime. What we might all agree on is that specific harmful human actions require punishment both to stop the perpetrator from committing similar acts again and to let the rest of the public know that such actions are not acceptable and will be punished again in the future. We must make every attempt to keep our biases in check when discussing this particular issue in as fair a light as possible. It is all too easy to get caught up in the emotional rhetoric that underlies the punishment of humans. Again, what we commonly share in our polarized positions on capital punishment is the reduction of harm. Just as innocent people are killed accidentally every year by gun violence, so too have innocent people been put to death by capital punishment. Is it worth the death of one single innocent person to justify the execution of 1,000 guilty others? There are no easy answers. But what we commonly share is that we want what's best for the victims of crime and for society at large.

SAME-SEX RELATIONSHIPS

The Extreme Polar Views

> Conservative: Sexual education and practice is something to be taught by parents to their children when they have reached the appropriate ages of maturity. Sexual education should not be taught in schools at any age level. Various sexual acts and information are considered to be unacceptable. Same-sex marriage is forbidden.
>
> Liberal: Sexual activity is a natural act. As such, it should be taught in schools at all levels according to the maturity and age of the students. Sexual freedom is tolerated provided that it take place between consenting adults. There is nothing immoral or illegal about same-sex marriage or same-sex acts.

When it comes to sexual education and practice, how do you define yourself? How liberal or conservative are you? Why do you have the beliefs you now do? What biases throughout your life have led you to this point in time to think about sex the way you now do? For those whose views are more conservative, there is often—though not always—an underlying element of religious belief. For example, the Abrahamic faiths—specifically fundamentalist Christian views, Orthodox Jewish, as well as Muslim views—place considerable emphasis on controlling one's sexual appetites. Sexual activity occurs between consenting adults—one male and one female. Same-sex activity is considered to be an abomination and therefore is forbidden and neither practiced, taught, nor tolerated. This has and continues to create considerable difficulty within some religious communities.

Many fundamentalist believers have considerable difficulty accepting that any of their children could be homosexual as opposed to heterosexual. This is because they believe that homosexuality—an act forbidden by God—to be a life choice, an act of free will, and hence a sin.

Liberals, on the other hand, often maintain that homosexuality is as natural a state as heterosexuality because it is largely the product of influences that are entirely beyond the person's control. Most liberals believe that homosexuality is the result of (among other things) biological and prenatal influences. As such, there is no choice or free will involved whatsoever. Therefore, they believe that to hold anyone morally accountable for being homosexual is unfair, unjust, and scientifically indefensible.

Common Ground

It must be extremely difficult for someone with strong religious faith to understand homosexuality in light of their belief system. On the one hand, you have your God telling you that homosexuality is a sin. On the other hand, your son or daughter turns out to be gay. Trying to reconcile one's supernatural beliefs with the sexuality of one's own offspring cannot be easy. But think of how many people have suffered ridicule, torture, and death and been ostracized in just the past few hundred years simply for being born with a different set of sexual biases. Yet, to a true believer, to believe that homosexuality is a choice and therefore sinful, worthy of condemning, ostracizing, castigating, and excommunicating a member of their faith, is internally consistent with their entire belief system. Unfortunately, it bears no external consistency to how the world actually functions. There is more than enough evidence, gathered from enough relevant sources, to give a clear indication of the high probability of a natural explanation for homosexuality.[2] This simply makes a true believer's understanding of homosexuality externally inconsistent.

The common ground in this unique case lies in the way in which we accept scientific information. For any true believer, to accept scientific information regarding the successful use of vaccinations or of the functional use of automobiles but not to accept it regarding human biological behavior, specifically that of human sexuality, is itself inconsistent. Yet I genuinely feel for those who have religious convictions that disallow them from understanding the natural state of being that is homosexuality. I know how difficult it must be for them to be faced with the decision between science and their God, and I can appreciate the cognitive dissonance that must result in feeling that they must choose between scientific discoveries and the commands of their God. But this, itself, may be a false dilemma. There are those who resolve the dilemma by considering how God's attributes could allow for homosexual behavior. For example, some maintain that it logically follows that if God created humans, who then developed the science of biology, and if the science of biology demonstrates that homosexuality is natural and that what God creates is natural, it must follow—or it entails—that God would not condemn homosexuality. To believe otherwise would be illogical.

There is also common ground in terms of the love parents have for their children and their desire not to see them harmed. We might want to consider to what extent parents would have to love their children more than their God in order to accept them as homosexuals. But clearly, my current biases influence me to state the conclusion that it is simply wrong to mistreat other human beings for any biological biases beyond their control. Since homosexuality is beyond anyone's control, it follows that it is simply wrong to mistreat people who are homosexual.[3]

And this leads us to a final area of common ground: the reduction of harm. Since we can all agree that people should not be punished for actions they have not committed or been responsible for, it must follow that it would be harmful to do so. Homosexuality is a state of being that was not chosen and therefore cannot exist as a punishable offense. If any belief system—religious or secular—mistreats or punishes people who happen to be homosexual, the actions must be addressed and stopped. In any society, we want people to have as much freedom as possible, and this includes religious freedom. But whether we are discussing religious freedom or secular freedom, what we would all agree on as common ground is the understanding that no belief system should be tolerated if its beliefs generate unwarranted harmful actions to other people or other species.

GOD/RELIGION—THEIST VERSUS ATHEIST

The Extreme Polar Views

> God exists: I know for sure that God exists and that my definition of him is 100 percent accurate and certain. Everyone who disagrees with me is wrong and will be punished eternally in the afterlife.

> God does not exist: I know for sure that no Gods exist. Belief in God and organized religions serve absolutely no purpose and should be banished.

Most people in the world (roughly five out of seven) believe in some sort of god. These gods are defined in quite a few different ways, making up more than 4,000 different types of religion. There are around 1 billion Hindus, 1.6 billion Muslims, and 2.2 billion Christians in the world. Does this mean that any particular god actually exists? Not necessarily. To believe so would commit the fallacy of popularity. As we saw earlier, it was once quite popular to believe that the earth was flat and that the sun revolved around it. Popularity alone does not produce truth. It follows, then, that it is logically and physically impossible for all the world religions to be correct. However, it is logically and physically possible for all of them to be wrong. So why, with so many people in the world believing in various gods, are there some who choose not to believe in any at all?

Atheists state that there is no real convincing evidence for belief in any particular god of any particular religious worldview. They distinguish between knowledge of the natural world and faith in supernatural beings. Knowledge of the natural world is gained through scientific investigation, rational discourse, and empirical understanding. Faith in supernatural beings has no appeal in the natural world and therefore can be neither falsified nor confirmed. Therefore, for atheists, it seems illogical and impractical to believe in things that are beyond empirical investigation.

For theists, however, their sense of spirituality is their greatest joy and produces their strongest set of beliefs. For many theists, their spiritual experiences are deeply personal, emotionally powerful, and not necessarily prone to empirical observation. So how do we disagree and get along?

Common Ground

Just as we saw in the consideration of common ground between liberals and conservatives in same-sex relationships, so too do we now find ourselves considering the amount of harm that natural versus supernatural beliefs generate. I think both theists and atheists can agree that people should be allowed to believe whatever they want with the very important proviso that such beliefs do not generate actions that cause harm to other people or other species. We value liberty and freedom of choice as well as freedom of conscience to believe and practice freely whatever we choose. However, no matter what our views are, it follows that, as a society, we should not have to tolerate unwarranted harmful actions caused by any belief system, whether theist or atheist, secular or religious.

This leads us to consider another area of common ground between theists and atheists: our shared values. Atheists and theists alike favor many human values and actions, such as friendship, loyalty, fidelity, trustworthiness, compassion, honesty, and so on. As it turns out, atheists pay their taxes just like theists do. Theists are hardworking, compassionate, and caring people, just as atheists are. Most often, one of the few major differences between the two is a belief in a single god. Other than that, both sides contain people just trying to live their lives in relative peace and comfort. I don't believe that theists love their children any less or any more than do atheists, and I don't believe that atheists care for the homeless any less or any more than do theists. People are generally judged by their actions. In the common ground between atheists and theists lie the values that are shared between both worldviews, making it easier to live in disagreement yet still get along.

PSEUDOSCIENCE AND PARANORMAL PHENOMENA

Defining the term *pseudoscience* can be problematic—but not because we don't know what it means. We do. The term *pseudo* comes from the Greek ψευδο, meaning "false." But the term takes on a wider meaning as "fake" or "not real" when we consider standard definitions:

- A system of theories, assumptions, and methods erroneously regarded as scientific[4]
- A pretended or spurious science; a collection of related beliefs about the world mistakenly regarded as being based on the scientific method or as having the status that scientific truths now have[5]

So it is a term that refers to "fake science." In other words, it seems like science; it uses science-like terms and protocols. But it lacks the ability either to be falsified as all other areas of scientific study can be or to produce predictions of novelty that elicit convincing evidence. As we shall see, there are many types of ideas that fall into the category of pseudoscience. The difficulty lies in how and when to place specific fields of inquiry into this category. Michael Shermer attempts to offer some help by stating what he calls a practical criterion for resolving the demarcation problem:

> . . . the conduct of scientists as reflected in the pragmatic usefulness of an idea. That is, does the revolutionary new idea generate any interest on the part of working scientists for adoption in their research programs, produce any new lines of research, lead to any new discoveries, or influence any existing hypotheses, models, paradigms or worldviews? If not, chances are it is pseudoscience.[6]

We have to be careful with Shermer's demarcation here, for there have been plenty of cases throughout history (e.g., the Psi Factor involving KGB and CIA agents potentially using telekinesis as a weapon, Lysenko-based agricultural theories in Russia, beliefs that Uri Geller could bend metal with his mind, and so on) that had the scientific community involved for years and spending millions of dollars investigating them. Granted, the scientific method eventually demonstrated that such phenomena were indeed pseudoscientific. But many of these ideas did comply with Shermer's first demarcation distinction insofar as they did generate interest—in some cases quite a lot of interest—with working scientists and were adopted in research programs that influenced existing hypotheses and so on.

Shermer then focuses on defining not so much what science is but rather what scientists do as a second demarcating point from pseudoscience:

> We can demarcate science from pseudoscience less by what science is and more by what scientists do. Science is a set of methods aimed at testing hypotheses and building theories. If a community of scientists actively adopts a new idea and if that idea then spreads through the field and is incorporated into research that produces useful knowledge reflected in presentations, publications, and especially new lines of inquiry and research, chances are it is science.[7]

Shermer's first sentence seems to belie his claim about what science is because he provides a very good definition in stating that science "is a set of methods aimed at testing hypotheses and building theories." He then proceeds to state that it is the popularity of ideas that makes information "scientific." Although I agree that, as we saw in chapter 6, the ad populum fallacy maintains that popularity is no guarantee of truth or acceptability, Shermer has overlooked the fact that the demarcation of science and pseudoscience can best be understood by considering how science actually works. We must never forget that the popularity of acceptable scientific ideas results only after rigorous methodology and replication. As we saw in considerable detail in chapter 5, scientific discoveries can result only after scientists rigorously adhere to the strict methodologies that have evolved and been refined over centuries of work.

This is what really demarcates or distinguishes science from pseudoscience: it's whether the scientific method has been faithfully followed, thus producing convincing evidence attained in a consistent, reliable, relevant, and sufficient manner. If the findings can be repeatedly replicated, we can agree—perhaps provisionally—that the findings are indeed scientific.

Now that we have greater clarity regarding the distinctions between science and pseudoscience, we can consider in some detail why it is irresponsible to believe in the truth of their claims.

In alphabetical order, some of the most well-known pseudoscientific subjects include astrology, Bigfoot, Christian Science, conversion therapy, crop circles, crystal healing, ghost hunting, homeopathy, levitation, the Loch Ness Monster, New Age healing, psychic phenomena (e.g., telekinesis, psychic readings, telepathy, clairvoyance, ESP, spirit channeling, and so on), Scientology, traditional Chinese medicine, and ufology. I have mentioned some of these in past chapters, so I will limit my analysis and time to those I think are the most troubling. Note that all of my critiques on the following pseudoscientific subjects are based on the condition that the information I have stated about them is accurate and true. If I am wrong or misguided in my presentation of these topics and have not stated them in a fair and accurate manner, then I must be willing to accept further evidence from those who believe in such ideas. Let's begin.

ASTROLOGY

There are several different types of astrology, depending on which part of the world one comes from. The type that concerns us here is a Western form known as natal astrology. A general definition of astrology can be defined as

> the study of the movements and positions of the sun, moon, planets, and stars in the belief that they affect the character and lives of people. *Unlike astronomy, astrology cannot be described as an exact science. In astrology, a person's personality is supposed to relate to which star sign they were born under.*[8]

So the argument for astrology maintains the conclusion that at the time of your birth, much of your personality and fate have been established according to the positions of various celestial objects. Okay. What are the premises in support of such a conclusion? Do these premises satisfy the universal foundational criteria of consistency, simplicity, relevance, reliability, and sufficiency?

Western astrology is generally made up of four components: planets, signs, houses, and a chart. We would maintain that each of these four components makes up major premises in the support of the conclusion of astrology. The following information comes from the best available source I could find: Kepler College. This college was established in 1999 in Seattle, Washington, and offers bachelor's and master's degrees in programs in "astrological studies."

In reference to planets, the college website states the following:

> The planets are the key actors in a chart. They represent a set of principles, functions of our psyche, or an archetypal energy. Astrological planets include the two lights (the Sun and Moon) and the visible planets Mercury through Saturn. Modern Western astrologers also use the more recently discovered planets of Uranus and Neptune. Most modern astrologers also include the dwarf planet Pluto because they have nearly 100 years of exploring its meaning.[9]

So there was a time in history when astrologers never even knew of other planets in our solar system. That should raise a few red flags of warning right there. Anyhow, let's look at their next major premise. With regard to signs, astrologers believe that

> the expression of the planets is modified through the astrological sign. The signs indicate a quality of action and are also categorized by the qualities of the four elements fire, earth, air and water. The astrological signs of the zodiac are not the same as the astronomical constellations, even though they share the same name. Astrological signs are a coordinate system like a map which divides the 360 degree circle of the ecliptic into 30 degree divisions.[10]

But what exactly does this mean? How are planets "modified through the astrological sign"? And why do the signs indicate a "quality of action characterized by the qualities of fire, earth, air, and water"? It would appear that the so-called evidence for belief in astrology is already beginning to violate the universal criterion of simplicity. In other words, the belief system seems to be multiplying entities far beyond what is necessary. But let's move on.

The third major premise involves houses:

> The astrological houses are calculated based on a specific time and place. The houses describe how a planet in a particular sign relates to different areas of life or fields of experience. The 12 astrological houses divide the chart based on the daily rotation of the earth.[11]

So how do houses get calculated in relation to a particular sign to different areas of life? I want to be able to better understand the more complete argument for astrology. However, it seems to be a complicated, convoluted, ambiguous way of trying to describe human personality. Still, the three components of planets, houses, and signs are plotted on a chart that is described as follows:

> The position of each of these symbols is plotted on a map called an astrological horoscope. The chart is interpreted based on the type of question being asked and the type of astrology the practitioner follows. There are many uses for an astrological chart.[12]

For natal astrology, the main use of the chart is to discover something about the psychology of an individual. So we are to believe that at the exact moment of one's birth, the way in which the sun, the moon, and the planets align according to houses and signs determines the type of person you will become. Should we believe this? Since we cannot scientifically test the *reliability* of the information behind the main premises, we are unable to determine their *relevance* to the conclusion. We have already seen that this argument far exceeds the bounds of *simplicity* and incorporates myriad complex and convoluted concepts and ideas. We can conclude the *sufficiency* of the premises is lacking and fails to convince me to accept the conclusion. Finally, we can easily demonstrate the overall lack of *consistency* of such a belief system. Several experiments have been conducted in which people have been asked to read descriptions of their personalities according to specific astrological signs. When asked to rank the accuracy of the description to one's personality, most people listed the description as being extremely accurate. The problem, however, is that the description was the same for all people involved in the study regardless of their astrological sign. One of the first experiments to test the accuracy of astrology occurred in 1948. Psychologist Bertram R. Forer conducted a psychology test called a "Diagnostic Interest Blank." He gave this test to thirty-nine psychology students who were told that they would each receive a personality analysis based on their test results. After a week, Forer gave each of the students a supposedly individual personality analysis and asked them to rate it on a scale of accuracy from 0 to 5. However, each student received the same personality analysis, which stated the following:

1. You have a great need for other people to like and admire you.
2. You have a tendency to be critical of yourself.
3. You have a great deal of unused capacity which you have not turned to your advantage.
4. While you have some personality weaknesses, you are generally able to compensate for them.
5. Your sexual adjustment has presented problems for you.
6. Disciplined and self-controlled outside, you tend to be worrisome and insecure inside.
7. At times you have serious doubts as to whether you have made the right decision or done the right thing.
8. You prefer a certain amount of change and variety and become dissatisfied when hemmed in by restrictions and limitations.

9. You pride yourself as an independent thinker and do not accept others' statements without satisfactory proof.
10. You have found it unwise to be too frank in revealing yourself to others.
11. At times you are extroverted, affable, sociable, while at other times you are introverted, wary, reserved.
12. Some of your aspirations tend to be pretty unrealistic.
13. Security is one of your major goals in life.[13]

Of the thirty-nine students, the average rate for accuracy was 4.3. Forer believed that the high scores were the result of human gullibility, and others have maintained that it confirms the *Pollyanna principle*, which means that we generally appreciate the use of positive words or feedback more than negative ones. This is often referred to as *subjective validation*. The same effect takes place with psychic readings as well. You're never going to hear a psychic tell one of their customers that they are an asshole. Nor will they tell them that they are morally retarded. They tell their customers what they want to hear.

Magician and educator James Randi has repeated this experiment many times and arrived at similar, very high percentages. Astrological readings are so vague that they could apply to just about anyone at any time. So there is very little value or purpose for astrology in modern culture. This is now known formally as the Forer effect or the Barnum effect. It is essentially a cognitive confirmation bias in which individuals believe that their astrological personality descriptions are highly accurate—mostly because of the flattering things that are said—and then believe such readings to have been devised specifically for them.

In an early episode of *The Big Bang Theory*, Penny tells Sheldon and Leonard that she is a Sagittarius, and that probably tells them far too much than they need to know about her, Sheldon replies, "Yes, it tells us that you participate in the mass cultural delusion that the sun's apparent position relative to arbitrarily defined constellations at the time of your birth, somehow affects your personality." To put things into perspective, consider the following: the cell phone you use every day exerts far more physical effect or energy on you than the moon, the planets, and the stars ever will. By measuring the effects of sources of energy in terms of gravitational, electromagnetic, and microwave radiation, we determine quite convincingly that the basis for astrology has been undermined.[14] There is no available evidence to indicate that such a belief in astrology is or has ever been warranted. Until such time, astrology must stay in the realm of the pseudosciences.

BIGFOOT

Bigfoot is defined as a Sasquatch, which is defined as

> A hairy creature like a human being reported to exist in the northwestern U.S. and western Canada and said to be a primate between 6 and 15 feet (1.8 and 4.6 meters) tall.[15]

So the conclusion is that a very large, bipedal, simian-like creature inhabits various parts of North America. The premises in support of such a conclusion include the following:

1. Footprints. "The mystery behind the sightings of sasquatches (a term used interchangeably with bigfoot) took on a new dimension in the 1960's when Dr. Grover Krantz of Washington State University began examining casts and photos of footprints from various parts of Washington. One of the sets of casts showed anatomical features of an injured foot that were either made by a real upright-walking primate, or an artist with an expert understanding of primate foot anatomy. . . . The footage has been repeatedly analyzed by scientists over the last 40 years. It has never been proven to be a hoax, yet various individuals have 'confessed' to being the man in the costume over the years. . . . The difficulty in creating a matching costume has to do with the limb ratios. The figure in the footage has shorter legs and larger arms, proportionally, than a human. The differences are most apparent when the figure is juxtaposed to the figure of a human in a Bigfoot costume."[16]

2. Recorded sounds: "There are many examples of recordings attributed to the sounds of Bigfoots, which are very distinct from the sounds of other animals. Bigfoots are said to make loud howls and screams at night, as well as wood knocking

sounds or rock clacking sounds. The most compelling collection of recordings was obtained in California's Sierra Nevada Mountains in the 1970's with the help of a newspaper journalist from Sacramento. Those recordings, called the 'Sierra Sounds' collection, are widely believed to be authentic recordings of bigfoots. A few of those recordings captured what sounds like a primitive language."[17]

3. Eyewitness accounts: "There are, in fact, way too many eyewitnesses for this phenomenon to be purely imaginary, as skeptics assert. With such an abundance of eyewitnesses, who are so dispersed across the continent, and dispersed across the decades, the alternate skeptical explanation that the sightings are the result of hoaxers, in whole or even in large part, becomes much less likely."[18]

4. Fuzzy video footage: The Patterson-Gimlin film is widely regarded as one of the strongest pieces of evidence for the existence of sasquatches."[19]

Each one of these main premises has been falsified. If you want to find ample counterevidence of this, there are many sources.[20] So there is no real, compelling reason to maintain a belief that such a creature is actually real.

In determining the apparent existence of such a creature through the pseudoscientific study known as cryptozoology, we may rightly ask a series of important questions. First, has the body of a Sasquatch ever been found? No. What about skeletal remains? No. Now, this creature is supposed to be quite large. That means that it is rational to infer that it will have a fairly large appetite, thereby generating fairly large amounts of waste. In other words, such a creature would take enormous dumps. If so, surely there has been scatological evidence for such a being? No. So what should we conclude? What is the responsible position to take regarding the supposed existence of such a being? Since the onus of responsibility is always on the claimant and no tangible evidence has yet been provided, the responsible position to take would be disbelief in the existence of so-called Bigfoot. Now, should someone, somehow, somewhere produce fact-based evidence for such a creature, we must be willing to change our views. However, until such a time, there is no need for anyone, anywhere, to believe that such a creature exists. Commit belief in such a creature to the dustbin of pseudoscience.

CHRISTIAN SCIENCE

When it comes to investigating pseudoscientific claims, no body of information is immune—including apparent religious beliefs. But what is Christian Science? How did it start?

> In about 1850, Phineas Parkhurst Quimby of Maine used Anton Mesmer's ideas of animal magnetism to develop his own healing approach. Quimby would place his hands on a sick patient's head and abdomen and encourage supposed magnetic healing forces to flow through them. He claimed that diagnosis and cure resulted from the individual's faith in him. He professed that conventional medicine was useless, that disease itself was "error," and that only health was "truth." In 1862, Quimby treated Mary Baker Glover for a spinal problem that had failed to respond to orthodox medical care. The water massage and hypnotism that he used reportedly had a positive effect. On awakening from her trance Glover found herself cured. She concluded, however, that her cure was not due to Quimby but to "truth in Christ." In 1875 she published *Science and Health*, which described her theories about religion based on the Bible and some of Quimby's ideas. She said that God was the author and that she was only the writer. In 1877 she married for the third time, becoming Mary Baker Eddy, and named her new philosophy Christian Science. The Church of Christ, Scientist was founded in 1879. Mary Baker Eddy represented herself as the supreme healer and as infallible as Christ. She claimed to be able to perform miracles and said she had healed many people with crippling disabilities. She demanded absolute obedience to her system as well as to her person. She could not bear to be contradicted or found wrong. In her determination to justify herself on all counts, she frequently twisted evidence and facts to her purposes. Her writings contain many contradictions.[21]

The basic conclusion of Christian Science is that physical ailments can be treated not through medical science but through prayer:

Christian Science contends that illness is an illusion caused by faulty beliefs, and that prayer heals by replacing bad thoughts with good ones. Christian Science practitioners work by trying to argue the sick thoughts out of the patient's mind. Consultations can take place in person, by telephone, or even by mail. Individuals may also be able to attain correct beliefs by themselves through prayer or concentration.[22]

The premise that illness is an illusion is a dangerous one that has led to the unfortunate pain, suffering, and deaths of many people—including children—who subscribed to such pseudoscientific beliefs:

Rita Swan, Ph.D., whose 16-month-old son Matthew died of meningitis in 1977 under the care of two Christian Science practitioners, quickly collected allegations of 75 deaths and 95 serious injuries to children of Christian Scientists. Angered by her experience, she formed Children's Healthcare Is a Legal Duty, Inc. (CHILD) to work for legal reforms that could protect children from inappropriate treatment by faith healers. She also sued the church but lost the case. During the proceedings, church officials testified that the church had no training, workshops, or meetings for practitioners that included any discussion on how to evaluate the seriousness of a child's condition. A 1993 lawsuit following the death of an 11-year-old boy resulted in a $1.5 million judgment against the boy's mother and stepfather and two Christian Science practitioners. Press reports indicate that the boy died after passing into diabetic coma while the mother prayed at his bedside and the practitioner took notes about his condition.[23]

There are several studies indicating that followers of Christian Science tend to live shorter lives than those who do not subscribe to its teachings. Note that there is nothing wrong per se in practicing religious beliefs guaranteed by any constitution to protect religious freedom. Our critical thinking skills and awareness and acceptance of the plurality of ideas within a given society inform us that we should be fair in the consideration of differing viewpoints based on differing biases. However, once beliefs—religious or otherwise—influence actions that generate harm, we have an obligation to speak up loudly and clearly and expose the inconsistent and contradictory beliefs for what they are: in this case, pseudoscience.

CONVERSION THERAPY

The definition of conversion therapy refers to

> the widely discredited practice that attempts to change a person's sexual orientation or gender identity. . . . Further defined during the late 1970s, the term conversion therapy began to be used for the process of attempting to turn gay people straight. . . . At this time, it was used exclusively to refer to attempts to change the sexual orientation of gay and lesbian people. . . . In 2014, a transgender teen, Leelah Alcorn committed suicide, explicitly citing conversion therapy as a motivating factor. The circumstances behind her suicide caused outrage across the country, which then Pres. Obama addressed. Conversion therapy was also linked to vice president Mike Pence during the 2016 election, as he was accused of funding its continuation with federal dollars.[24]

So the conclusion of conversion therapy is that you can successfully change or convert the sexual preference of men and women through a particular process. You can see why a deeply religious person might believe conversion therapy as being internally consistent with their particular views. If I believe the Bible tells me that homosexuality is a sin, then I might find it quite consistent that *choosing* homosexuality as a lifestyle choice can be altered and changed in a human being. But as we saw earlier in considering same-sex relationships, the problem with this reasoning is that it treats homosexuality as a choice. But the most current evidence-based findings in the fields of biology and human sexuality clearly demonstrate that it is not. We now know quite clearly that homosexuality is as much a choice as is heterosexuality, bisexuality, or even pedophilia. One's sexual orientation is hardwired and is simply beyond a person's *choice*. There may not be a specific, so-called gay gene, but there is overwhelming evidence that clearly demonstrates that there are strong biological factors at work.

Hence, it follows that trying to convert someone from their so-called choice of sexual orientation is scientifically unfounded and remains in the realm of the pseudosciences. Therefore, it would be epistemically and morally irresponsible to believe that conversion therapy is true.

GHOST HUNTING

About a decade or so ago, I was contacted by a producer from a television network who wanted me to host a show that debunked paranormal phenomena like psychics, ghosts, Bigfoot, UFOs, and so on. During the interview and development process, I was informed that the show would take on a type of *Myth Busters* approach to various pseudoscientific claims. I was both excited and encouraged to be involved in a program that I believed would be of considerable value in informing the public about fallacious ideas. So, as I was thinking about content for various episodes and deciding on which pseudoscientific topic I might investigate first, I received a short but telling e-mail from the producer telling me that the idea had been canceled and that they were going in a new direction. A short time later, I found out that the direction they were heading involved the development of a show for "ghost hunters." The perceived likelihood of better ratings called for a show involving people in search of ghosts in apparent haunted houses and establishments. I found this to be very telling not only of what television executives saw as dollar signs but also in realizing that the general public was far more interested in being entertained with nonsense than illuminated with knowledge. This is not simply a case of sour grapes. I really don't care if I have a television show. What I do care about is informing the public about true information. Not only is creating a show about ghost hunting diametrically opposed to the original show they were planning to air, but in so doing, the television network is spreading false information about beings that do not exist in an attempt to gain higher ratings and make more money. Personally and professionally, I find such tactics beneath contempt.

The bottom line is this: no one has ever demonstrated the existence of ghosts. Until they do, the responsible position to take is that they do not exist. If they did exist, we should be able to find them and repeatedly demonstrate their existence. However, the so-called ghost hunters have not been able to provide a single shred of evidence for their existence. Until such a time that such actual, fact-based evidence can be brought forward, the idea of ghosts and the practice of ghost hunting will remain in the realm of the pseudosciences.

HOMEOPATHY

For those of you who do not know what homeopathy is or how it is supposed to work, here is a brief description. Whenever you think of homeopathy, remember the phrase "dilution is the solution." The word *homeopathy* is derived from the Greek words *homoios*, for "similar," and *pathos*, for "suffering" or "disease." It was founded by Samuel Hahnemann (1755–1843), a German physician, in the late 1700s. Hahnemann developed a theory called the "law of similars," which involved the idea that symptoms of various diseases could be cured by administering very small amounts of substances that cause negative symptoms in healthy people when administered in large amounts:

> Hahnemann declared that diseases represent a disturbance in the body's ability to heal itself and that only a small stimulus is needed to begin the healing process. He also claimed that chronic diseases were manifestations of a suppressed itch (*psora*), a kind of miasma or evil spirit. At first he used small doses of accepted medications. But later he used enormous dilutions and theorized that the smaller the dose, the more powerful the effect—a notion commonly referred to as the "law of infinitesimals." That, of course, is just the opposite of the dose-response relationship that pharmacologists have demonstrated.[25]

So how are such "infinitesimals" made?

> Homeopathic products are made from minerals, botanical substances, and several other sources. If the original substance is soluble, one part is diluted with either nine or ninety-nine parts of distilled water and/or alcohol and shaken vigorously (succussed); if insoluble, it is finely ground and pulverized in similar proportions with powdered lactose (milk sugar). One part of the diluted medicine is then further diluted, and the process is repeated until the desired concentration is reached. Dilutions of 1 to 10 are designated by the Roman numeral X (1X = 1/10, 3X = 1/1,000, 6X = 1/1,000,000). Similarly, dilutions of 1 to 100 are designated by the Roman numeral C (1C = 1/100, 3C = 1/1,000,000, and so on). Most remedies today range from 6X to 30X, but products of 30C or more are marketed.

A 30X dilution means that the original substance has been diluted 1,000,000,000,000,000,000,000,000,000,000 times. Assuming that a cubic centimeter of water contains 15 drops, this number is greater than the number of drops of water that would fill a container more than 50 times the size of the Earth. Imagine placing a drop of red dye into such a container so that it disperses evenly. Homeopathy's "law of infinitesimals" is the equivalent of saying that any drop of water subsequently removed from that container will possess an essence of redness.[26]

When you do the math, it becomes clear that those who take homeopathic tinctures are really just ingesting water. The same infinitesimally minute dosage will be found in pill form as well. This leads us to consider whether it is ethical to sell a product that does absolutely nothing in the guise that it is helping people in some way. Aside from the obvious placebo effect of people convincing themselves that such quackery actually works, there can be no real benefit gained from such so-called medicine.

In 2015, the Australian government's National Health and Research Council produced a forty-page report that concluded that homeopathic treatment is worthless. After surveying the scientific literature, the authors said the following:

- Based on all the evidence considered, there were no health conditions for which there was reliable evidence that homeopathy was effective.
- No good-quality, well-designed studies with enough participants for a meaningful result reported either that homeopathy caused greater health improvements than placebo, or caused health improvements equal to those of another treatment.
- Homeopathy should not be used to treat conditions that are chronic, serious, or could become serious.
- People who choose homeopathy may put their health at risk if they reject or delay treatments for which there is good evidence for safety and effectiveness.
- People who are considering whether to use homeopathy should first get advice from a registered health practitioner. Those who use homeopathy should tell their health practitioner, and should keep taking any prescribed treatments.[27]

Both the epistemic and ethical position to take on homeopathy is to leave it in the realm of the pseudosciences. It should harken us back to Hume's and Clifford's advice proportioning ourselves to the evidence and maintaining that it is wrong always, everywhere, and for anyone to believe anything on insufficient evidence. Not only does homeopathy as a belief system fail epistemically and scientifically, it also fails ethically as well. Unless and until there is better evidence coming from double-blind studies, don't waste your money, for no person should ever condone the practice of homeopathy knowing of its misguided and false claims. To do so would be unethical. This is why Clifford would have referred to this type of example as a violation of the "ethics of belief." In other words, people *ought not* to believe in any effects from homeopathic treatment. We have a duty to refuse it based on its lack of evidence. To do otherwise would be the result of a lack of discernment gained through the proper use of the critical thinking skill set.

PSYCHIC PHENOMENA

As I mentioned earlier, psychic phenomena can refer to a number of different claims involving such things as telekinesis, psychic readings, telepathy, clairvoyance, ESP, spirit channeling, and so on. To cut to the chase, it's all nonsense. None of it is true, and none of it has been demonstrated under the slightest of scientific standards. If any of it were true, there would be ample evidence to prove it. But when we look for supporting premises, there is no evidence to prove it—not even in the slightest. So we are therefore justified in maintaining that none of it is true. Should any evidence emerge, then, as responsible critical thinkers, we must set aside any preexisting biases against psychic phenomena and follow where the evidence leads us. If it leads to the conclusion that some form of psychic phenomena has been demonstrated, then we would have little choice but to believe it. I'm still waiting; you're still waiting; we're all still waiting. But, sadly, while we're all waiting, millions continue to attend "psychic fairs" every year and waste their hard-earned money. In 2018, total revenue for psychics in the United States surpassed $2 billion. What drives this ship are two essential elements: hope and ignorance. People seek out psychic help hoping for a better future but are simply ignorant of the fact that they are being swindled.

There have been studies, tests, and various attempts to allow psychic practitioners to demonstrate their abilities. All have failed. But educate yourselves on this subject. There is an organization called the Committee for the Scientific Investigation of Claims of the Paranormal.[28] This group is made up of scientists, philosophers, medical doctors, magicians, and so on who devote their time to "debunking" people who lay claim to "paranormal" phenomena. Why do they wish to debunk such claims? Because they feel they have an epistemic responsibility to inform the public when they are being swindled and scammed. Many of our beliefs in strange occurrences are usually erroneous if not, at least, unfounded. Most of the fallacious reasoning responsible for these types of erroneous beliefs is due to the fallacy of argumentum ad ignorantiam. People often make the following appeal to various fields of the paranormal:

(P1) Scientists haven't proven astrology (or ESP, psychic readings, and so on), <u>to be false</u>.

(C) Therefore, they must be true.

As we have seen, when anyone appeals to ignorance in this type of way, they can justify just about any claim—like Santa Claus, the Easter Bunny, or the Tooth Fairy. Whenever anyone makes such an extraordinary claim, it is their responsibility to prove this by providing the extraordinary evidence. So it's *show me the money* time! Whenever anyone makes such a claim, the onus of responsibility lies with them to convince us. Otherwise, we can justify practically any belief, such as that there are exactly twelve purple elephants eating pink popcorn on the dark side of the moon right now. How do I know this? I have special psychic powers. Can I prove this? No. But then, again, you cannot disprove it, so it must be true. To consider the falsity of psychic phenomena, there is an overwhelming amount of literature and material available at your disposal.[29] In addition, the James Randi Education Foundation has hosted large conferences every year in Las Vegas that invited speakers from around the world to discuss various forms of pseudoscientific and psychic phenomena. Every year at these events, James Randi would host a "One Million Dollar Paranormal Challenge":

> The One Million Dollar Paranormal Challenge was an offer by the James Randi Educational Foundation (JREF) to pay out one million U.S. dollars to anyone who could demonstrate a supernatural

or paranormal ability under agreed-upon scientific testing criteria. A version of the challenge was first issued in 1964. Over a thousand people applied to take it, but none were successful. The challenge was terminated in 2015.[30]

I was fortunate enough to be invited to speak at several of these events. The enthusiasm and spirit of the speakers and attendees was encouraging. It was an excellent series of conferences in the promotion of critical thinking, and I think James Randi's passionate legacy for critical thinking is one that, it is hoped, will permeate through the education systems not only in the United States but around the world as well.

Now some readers might be thinking to themselves, "Oh, lighten up DiCarlo; psychics just give people hope for a better future—even if they are just playing on the Forer effect." For some, that might be the case. But here are a few things you need to know. Anyone claiming to be a psychic has no special powers. Either they are deluded into believing they have such special powers, or they are simply lying. More often than not, it's probably the latter. Still, I could teach anyone, anywhere, any time to be as convincing a psychic as you will ever go to. It's not that difficult. You start with generalities about a person, for example, that they're well liked, that they feel lonely sometimes, that they wish they were more successful, that they wish they had more money, that they're about to go on a trip, that they just came home from a trip, or any other form of generality, and because of confirmation bias, the person listening will often focus more on the times you were right than on the times you were wrong. Even if you were wrong 90 percent of the time, once you are right 10 percent of the time, you now know something about that person, from which you can make other so-called psychic claims. Eventually, depending on the gullibility and need of the person with whom you're speaking, you are likely to convince someone that you have some sort of special gift when in fact you do not. Remember, nobody ever goes to a psychic to be told they have nothing to look forward to in their future. All psychics tell you what you want to hear. They prey on ignorance and vulnerability, and they capitalize on hope for a better future. When I have taught critical thinking courses at various universities in my life, I have extended invitations to psychics every year to come into my class to demonstrate the truthfulness of their "gifts." In more than twenty years, only one psychic accepted my challenge. By the time the class was finished, the psychic was convinced that there were other plausible explanations for the types of phenomena she believed in so fervently. She actually left my classroom grateful that she was given the opportunity to see what her biases were and how she could allow counterevidence to persuade her that her views about the paranormal might be false. She was the exception, and my class benefited greatly from her ability to accept counterevidence. But she was the exception. I'm going to leave you with a powerful example of why I tend to dislike people who make psychic claims of any kind. It involves a story of a woman named Amanda Berry. Berry was one of three women who were held captive in a house owned by a man named Ariel Castro. The women were often raped and chained to their bedsides and kept captive for more than ten years. In a book titled *Hope: A Memoir of Survival in Cleveland*, Berry and fellow captive Gina DeJesus wrote of their ordeals as sex slaves to Castro. On one particular day, Berry had learned that her mother, Louwana Miller, would be on the *Montel Williams Show* to meet with one of the world's most famous psychics, Sylvia Browne. In her diary, Berry's entry for November 16, 2004, was the following:

> This is huge! Mom's going to be on *The Montel Williams Show* . . . she's going to be on tomorrow with Sylvia Browne, that cool psychic. I love her. This is amazing! Mom and I used to watch Montel all the time and we loved it when Sylvia was on. She made some amazing predictions . . . I want my mom to know I'm alive. Sylvia has to tell her.[31]

It did not take long for Berry to realize, in the most shocking and horrific manner possible, that one of her heroes, Sylvia Browne, was a complete fake. For her November 17, 2004, diary entry, Berry wrote,

> There she is! . . . This is so exciting! Sylvia is asking mom about a "Cuban-looking" guy who is short and stocky. It's him! He's Puerto Rican, not Cuban, but it's close. "Can you tell me if they'll ever find her?" Mom asks. "Is she out there?" Then Sylvia says: "I hate this when they're in water. I just hate this. She's not alive, honey." What? Why did she say that? Mom's face just drops. I start crying and shouting at the TV. I'm not dead! I'm alive and I'm right here! . . . She is a fraud. Now my poor mother is going to be convinced I'm dead, because she trusts Sylvia. This is going to crush her. She has to ignore what she was told and keep believing I'm alive and fighting to bring me home. If she doesn't how can I keep hoping?[32]

It is difficult to imagine of a worse possible way of finding out that psychics are scammers. You may still think that, in most cases, psychics are harmless. But like hypocrites, they too vary only by degree and admission. As horrific as this appears, Berry's entry for December 5, 2004, is incredibly sad and heart wrenching:

> My mom's been on the news a lot and she seems different, sadder. She says she took down the yellow ribbons at our house. . . . Took down the posters in my room and gave away my computer. . . . All because of Sylvia Browne; that fake. She put a knife right in my mom's heart because it made for good TV ratings the article [in *The Plain Dealer*] says my mom is 98% sure that what Sylvia told her as true, but I'm dead. But she said she "lost it" after that show. I am crying so hard that I'm shaking. I wish God would show her some sort of sign that I'm alive. I get my strength from knowing that my mom is fighting for me. If she gives up, I'll feel like I don't exist.[33]

When Berry tuned into the *Montel Williams Show* that day, she watched in horror as the psychic Sylvia Browne told her mother, "She's not alive, honey. Your daughter's not the kind who wouldn't call." Louwana Miller was devastated to hear this news. Just over a year later, Louwana Miller was dead at the age of forty-four from apparent heart failure. Miller's friends told the media that her meeting with Browne was so devastating to her that she never recovered from hearing that news. Although Montel Williams offered a sort of apology to Berry stating that he was sorry if anything that was said on his show caused her pain. However, it does not excuse him from having psychics and other forms of pseudoscientific nonsense on his show. As for Browne, she died in 2013 having never apologized for any of her misleading predictions.

The next time anyone tells you psychics, clairvoyants, or spirit channelers are real or harmless, you tell them why Amanda Berry doesn't think so. Let's never forget this. For the love of reason and compassion, let's never forget this.

UFOS

Do UFOs exist? Of course they do. By definition, they are unidentified flying objects. There have been thousands of sightings of UFOs.

But that's not surprising. The real question to ask is this: after they are identified, are they extraterrestrial beings from other planets? Full disclosure: I want aliens to be real. I think one of the greatest events any human could ever experience would be to meet an actual alien from another planet. I am a huge science fiction fan. And in siding with the Drake equation, I would go so far as to say that, given the immense size of our universe, the likelihood that there are other existing forms of intelligent life somewhere else in the universe is probably quite good.[34] However, it does not mean that they have visited our planet or ever will. They may have. But I still haven't seen any overwhelmingly convincing evidence to believe this.

Some of you may remember an interesting Internet event meme inviting people to meet at Area 51 to find out what those government folks are really up to. At 12:00 p.m. on September 20, 2019, hundreds of thousands of people agreed to storm Area 51. On a Facebook page, more than 2 million people declared that they were willing to do so. Although this was intended to be an Internet hoax—more likely to sell merchandise than to mobilize the masses—a few hundred people did show up.[35] They didn't rush the gates of Area 51 like running anime characters. Instead, they just had a party.

I am just as interested and excited to find convincing evidence that aliens not only exist but also have visited our planet. But even after all of the millions of sightings of UFOs, not one of those sightings has produced in any way convincing evidence to believe that, once identified, that flying object is in fact an alien spaceship carrying extraterrestrial beings. I hold great hope for the future of our planet and the potential for one day meeting beings from another world. But wishing and hoping do not make facts, and so far, the lack of facts is quite telling. I *want* to be convinced that aliens walk among us. I'm almost convinced that my neighbor is one. But without warranted, relevant evidence gained in a reliable and responsible manner that is both consistent and sufficient, I am not convinced of the argument's conclusion, so I must remain unconvinced of the existence of aliens visiting and perhaps staying on our planet. The most responsible epistemic position to take regarding the existence of UFOs and aliens is to suspend judgment until such a time that the evidence convinces us otherwise.

Epilogue

*I*t was my overall intention to provide the reader with some of the most important tools of the critical thinking skill set. But it is not enough just to know what these tools are; they are intended to be used—every day and in all walks of life. I hope that in the future, with the fair use of these critical thinking tools, you will have become more empowered and considerate in the ways in which you have conversations. Every day, we are inundated with information coming from multiple sources. In the future, it will become increasingly more difficult to determine what information most closely resembles the truth. Without a firm grasp of the tools in the critical thinking skill set, we will be less able to make such discernments so that we can formulate informed opinions on important issues. Through the fair and proper use of these tools, we will come to have more intelligent conversation about important issues and in a civilized manner be more comfortable in practicing what C. S. Lewis called the art of disagreement. I've made it fairly clear that critical thinking is not easy. If it were, everyone would be doing it. It takes time, and it takes a great deal of effort. But above all, it requires us to embrace the concept of fairness in its application. If we truly value freedom of thought and expression and the free interplay and exchange of ideas, then we must do so through the continued practice and use of critical thinking skills. So by all means, let us have impassioned dialogue about issues that mean the most to us. Let our opinions and biases clash, let our differences of opinions be heard, but let us also grow thicker skins that will allow us to openly disagree with the wisdom to allow us to get along.

Notes

INTRODUCTION

1. https://en.oxforddictionaries.com/word-of-the-year/word-of-the-year-2016.
2. Thank you, Kellyanne Conway: https://www.youtube.com/watch?v=VSrEEDQgFc8.
3. From the Jewish Virtual Library: http://www.jewishvirtuallibrary.org/jsource/Holocaust/goebbelslie.html.
4. See https://www.eurekalert.org/pub_releases/2019-08/afps-fnc081919.php.
5. See Colin Klein, Peter Clutton, and Adam G. Dunn, Pathways to Conspiracy: The Social and Linguistic Precursors of Involvement in Reddit's Conspiracy Theory Forum, https://journals.plos.org/plosone/article?id=10.1371/journal.pone.0225098.
6. This joke has been said by a lot of comedians. I'm going to nod my head in the direction of Dennis Miller for this one.

CHAPTER 1

1. See H. K. Burgoon and J. L. Hale, Nonverbal Expectancy Violations: Model Elaboration and Application to Immediacy Behaviors, *Communication Monographs* 55 (1988): 58–79. doi:10.1080/03637758809376158.
2. https://science.howstuffworks.com/innovation/edible-innovations/breatharian1.htm.
3. https://science.howstuffworks.com/innovation/edible-innovations/breatharian1.htm.

4. http://time.com/4321036/donald-trump-bs.

5. And probably long before then.

6. Sophistry is the use of clever but false arguments, especially with the intention of deceiving (https://en.oxforddictionaries.com/definition/sophistry).

7. No matter what Brooke Shields or Kristen Bell tells you.

8. This run-on sentence was done intentionally to demonstrate a bit of President Trump's style of communication. To know what I mean, reread it in President Trump's voice.

9. https://www.aljazeera.com/news/2018/10/trump-mocks-christine-blasey-ford-kavanaugh-allegations-181003124844955.html.

10. https://plato.stanford.edu/entries/ockham/#4.1.

11. A phrase that apparently was never once uttered by Conan Doyle's character Sherlock Holmes. There are several instances, however, where he does say, "Exactly, my dear Watson."

12. For those unfamiliar with Catholicism, confession is an action that takes place between a parishioner of the Catholic faith and a priest. The parishioner confesses his or her sins in what is called a confessional—a type of booth within a church where the identity of the parishioner is kept secret from the priest. The priest then offers forgiveness, and the person often must do a type of penance in order to be forgiven for sinning.

13. For those interested, this particular structure is one of Aristotle's famous syllogisms of formal logic called *modus ponens*.

14. The major cause of such infections is due to *Streptococcus pyogenes*, which is most commonly found in the throats and noses of healthy carriers.

CHAPTER 2

1. See https://www.huffingtonpost.com/rick-clemons/frankly-my-deargay-men-ma_b_10806572.html.

2. See http://www.whatisepigenetics.com/what-is-epigenetics.

3. https://elifesciences.org/articles/19886.

4. https://www.theguardian.com/books/2015/jan/23/the-brains-way-healing-stories-remarkable-recoveries-norman-doidge-review.

5. https://www.ncbi.nlm.nih.gov/pmc/articles/PMC3181608.

6. https://www.nytimes.com/2007/02/06/us/06cnd-astronaut.html. We later learned that she had only purchased the diapers and was not actually wearing them.

7. https://www.independent.co.uk/news/uk/crime/nine-in-ten-murders-are-committed-by-men-research-finds-a7095861.html.

8. https://medicalxpress.com/news/2018-10-gender-schizophrenia.html. The original study can be found at https://doi.org/0.1080/17470919.201815 36613.

9. https://pewrsr.ch/2mlL5S9.

10. https://www.goodreads.com/quotes/76-a-lie-can-travel-half-way -around-the-world-while. Of course, this very quote is quite possibly not from Twain. See https://www.nytimes.com/2017/04/26/books/famous-misquotat ions.html. So let's be careful about how we receive and either accept or reject information.

11. A feeling of unease that upsets what I have called *memetic equilibrium*. See https://en.wikipedia.org/wiki/Memetics.

CHAPTER 3

1. See https://blacklivesmatter.com/about/herstory.

2. See https://www.kqed.org/mindshift/54470/why-content-knowledge -is-crucial-to-effective-critical-thinking. See also https://education.nsw.gov .au/media/exar/How-to-teach-critical-thinking-Willingham.pdf.

3. The episode first aired on September 15, 1967, and was called "Amok Time." It was also the first episode that introduces Spock's famous hand gesture indicating "Live long and prosper."

4. For example, https://www.washingtonpost.com/graphics/2018/world/ yemen-famine-crisis/?noredirect=on&utm_term=.275f0dd0cdcd.

5. https://learning.blogs.nytimes.com/2013/12/13/skills-practice-distin guishing-between-fact-and-opinion.

6. http://www.journalism.org/2018/06/18/distinguishing-between-factual -and-opinion-statements-in-the-news.

7. See also https://www.snopes.com, https://webliteracy.pressbooks.com/ chapter/fact-checking-sites, https://mediabiasfactcheck.com/2016/07/20/the-10 -best-fact-checking-sites, https://civilination.org/resources-old/fact-checking- sites, https://domainbigdata.com, and https://www.youtube.com/channel/UC4 B40JtdvMlyB637F1FnsQw.

8. https://www.youtube.com/watch?v=f6bkahREkzk.

9. https://www.chicagotribune.com/news/ct-viz-jussie-smollett-incident -night-details-htmlstory.html.

10. https://www.nbcnews.com/news/us-news/chicago-mayor-rahm-emanuel -police-chief-slam-prosecutors-dropping-jussie-n987566.

11. For more on this, see https://politicsandculture.org/2010/04/27/how -problem-solving-and-neurotransmission-in-the-upper-paleolithic-led-to-the

-emergence-and-maintenance-of-memetic-equilibrium-in-contemporary-world
-religions.

CHAPTER 4

1. https://ca.yahoo.com/news/donald-trump-said-wind-turbines-21295
3433.html.
2. https://www.greenfieldadvisors.com; "Do Wind Turbines Lower Property Values?," https://forbes.com.
3. https://www.niehs.nih.gov/health/topics/agents/emf/index.cfm.
4. Scott R. Loss and Peter P. Mara, Estimates of Bird Collision Mortality at Wind Facilities in the Contiguous United States, *Biological Conservation* 168 (December 2013): 201–9.
5. Wendy Koch, Wind Turbines Kill Fewer Birds Than Do Cats, Cell Towers, *USA Today*, September 15, 2014.

CHAPTER 5

1. Originally published in *Contemporary Review* (January 1877), reprinted in William Kingdon Clifford, *Lectures and Essays by the Late William Kingdon Clifford, F.R.S.*, 2nd ed., edited by Leslie Stephen and Frederick Pollock, with an introduction by F. Pollock (London: Macmillan, 1886), 344.
2. For a comprehensive examination of the history and application of this equation, see David Bodanis, $E=mc^2$: *A Biography of the World's Most Famous Equation* (New York: Berkley Books, 2000).
3. https://www.tylervigen.com/spurious-correlations.
4. I am aware of the ethical problem surrounding the use of animals in clinical experiments. The point here is to understand that they are sometimes used because they are considered to be good analogies for human subjects. Woven into this, of course, is the view that it is ultimately more acceptable to experiment on animals than humans in some circumstances. There is no easy solution to this. The arguments for or against such treatment can be stated in three ways. Either animals do not have rights, and we can do whatever we want to them; they have rights, just not those on par with humans, so we can do some things to them; or they have the *same* rights as humans, and we have no right to use them in such experiments at all regardless of how many human lives could be saved. Consider your argument carefully on whether you believe animals should be used for medical testing.

5. http://www.nature.com/news/over-half-of-psychology-studies-fail-reproducibility-test-1.18248.

6. https://www.theguardian.com/science/occams-corner/2013/sep/17/scientific-studies-wrong.

7. See *New Negatives in Plant Science* (https://www.journals.elsevier.com/new-negatives-in-plant-science), *Registered Reports: A Step Change in Scientific Publishing* (https://www.elsevier.com/reviewers-update/story/innovation-in-publishing/registered-reports-a-step-change-in-scientific-publishing), and *All Trials Campaign* (http://www.alltrials.net).

8. To learn more about native advertising, read this excellent article by Dan Shewan: https://www.wordstream.com/blog/ws/2014/07/07/native-advertising-examples.

9. D. L. Sackett, Bias in Analytic Research, *Journal of Chronic Diseases* 32 (1979): 51–63.

10. David J. Roy et al., *Bioethics in Canada* (Scarborough: Prentice Hall, 1994), 329.

11. https://www.urbandictionary.com/define.php?term=truthiness.

12. http://www.washingtonpost.com/wp-dyn/content/article/2010/10/01/AR2010100105262.html.

CHAPTER 6

1. See Daniel Dale's work on this as the Washington bureau chief for the *Toronto Star* at https://www.thestar.com/news/donald-trump-fact-check.html.

2. https://www.salon.com/2015/04/11/bill_clintons_surprising_faith_from_childhood_through_monica_lewinsky_the_real_story_of_the_presidents_belief_in_god.

3. http://rationalwiki.org/wiki/Godwin's_Law.

4. I sincerely hope this is a hoax. As publication of this book approaches, it appears that Shaquille O'Neal has now joined the flat-earthers of the NBA.

5. See https://www.forbes.com/sites/startswithabang/2017/11/24/five-impossible-facts-that-would-have-to-be-true-if-the-earth-were-flat/#322954407c4f.

6. http://begthequestion.info.

7. Thank you, *Caddyshack*.

8. http://www.dictionary.com/browse/theory.

9. For example, Directive 65/65/EEC1 (Europe) and the Kefauver Harris Amendment (United States). Stricter rules were developed and enforced in the United States by the Food and Drug Administration that required evidence indicating the effectiveness of drugs and statements as to whether any side effects

were detected during testing. This led to the Drug Efficacy Study Implementation, which retroactively reclassified drugs that were on the shelves at the time.

10. This is example is taken from an old friend and past professor of mine from the University of Guelph, Bill Hughes.

11. https://www.who.int/immunization/newsroom/new-measles-data-august-2019/en.

12. It Takes a Village Idiot and I Married One, *Family Guy*, season 5, episode 17, production no. 5ACX12 (first aired May 13, 2007).

13. For an excellent account of the O.J. Simpson trial, see the television series The People v. O. J. Simpson: American Crime Story.

14. Thank you, Joe Flaherty.

15. Since 2016, in Canada, this is now referred to as medical assistance in dying (MAID). Currently, in the United States, nine states (and Washington, D.C.) have legalized physician-assisted suicide: California, Colorado, Hawaii, Maine, Montana, New Jersey, Oregon, Vermont, and Washington.

CHAPTER 7

1. Thanks, Bruce.

2. See https://www.oxfordscholarship.com/view/10.1093/acprof:oso/978019 9838820.001.0001/acprof-9780199838820 and https://psycnet.apa.org/record/ 2011-25953-000.

3. This argument satisfies all five of the universal foundational criteria.

4. https://www.merriam-webster.com/dictionary/pseudoscience.

5. https://plato.stanford.edu/entries/pseudo-science.

6. https://www.scientificamerican.com/article/what-is-pseudoscience.

7. https://www.scientificamerican.com/article/what-is-pseudoscience.

8. https://dictionary.cambridge.org/dictionary/english/astrology.

9. https://keplercollege.org/courses/mod/book/view.php?id=1914& chapterid=172.

10. https://keplercollege.org/courses/mod/book/view.php?id=1914& chapterid=172.

11. https://keplercollege.org/courses/mod/book/view.php?id=1914& chapterid=172.

12. https://keplercollege.org/courses/mod/book/view.php?id=1914& chapterid=172.

13. https://en.wikipedia.org/wiki/Barnum_effect.

14. For an interesting treatment attempting to falsify the main premises, see https://www.universetoday.com/52219/debunking-astrology-mars-cant-influence-you.

15. https://www.merriam-webster.com/dictionary/Sasquatch.

16. http://www.animalplanet.com/tv-shows/finding-bigfoot/lists/bigfoot-evidence.

17. http://www.animalplanet.com/tv-shows/finding-bigfoot/lists/bigfoot-evidence.

18. http://www.animalplanet.com/tv-shows/finding-bigfoot/lists/bigfoot-evidence.

19. http://www.animalplanet.com/tv-shows/finding-bigfoot/lists/bigfoot-evidence.

20. See https://www.sciencenews.org/blog/gory-details/finally-some-solid-science-bigfoot, https://blogs.scientificamerican.com/tetrapod-zoology/if-bigfoot-were-real, https://video.nationalgeographic.com/video/00000144-0a3e-d3cb-a96c-7b3f24c90000, and https://exemplore.com/cryptids/Why-Bigfoot-is-Fake-Bigfoot-Debunked.

21. https://www.quackwatch.org/01QuackeryRelatedTopics/cs2.html.

22. https://www.quackwatch.org/01QuackeryRelatedTopics/cs2.html.

23. https://www.quackwatch.org/01QuackeryRelatedTopics/cs2.html.

24. https://www.dictionary.com/e/slang/conversion-therapy. See also https://www.britannica.com/topic/Christian-Science/Significance.

25. https://www.quackwatch.org/01QuackeryRelatedTopics/homeo.html.

26. https://www.quackwatch.org/01QuackeryRelatedTopics/homeo.html.

27. https://www.quackwatch.org/01QuackeryRelatedTopics/homeo.html.

28. Their website is http://www.csicop.org.

29. Consider, for example, *Flim-Flam!* by James Randi, *Why People Believe Weird Things* by Michael Shermer, *Spook* by Mary Roach, and *The Psychology of the Psychic* by David Marks.

30. https://en.wikipedia.org/wiki/One_Million_Dollar_Paranormal_Challenge.

31. https://friendlyatheist.patheos.com/2015/05/02/amanda-berry-on-the-despair-of-watching-a-tv-psychic-tell-your-mom-youre-dead.

32. https://friendlyatheist.patheos.com/2015/05/02/amanda-berry-on-the-despair-of-watching-a-tv-psychic-tell-your-mom-youre-dead.

33. https://friendlyatheist.patheos.com/2015/05/02/amanda-berry-on-the-despair-of-watching-a-tv-psychic-tell-your-mom-youre-dead.

34. See https://www.seti.org/drake-equation-index.

35. https://www.nytimes.com/2019/09/20/us/area-51-raid.html.

Bibliography

Aristotle. *De Interpretatione* and *Prior Analytics*. In *The Complete Works of Aristotle*, edited by Jonathan Barnes. Princeton, NJ: Princeton University Press, 1984.

Barnett, Bronwyn. Genetics May Help Solve Mysteries of Human Evolution. Stanford News Service, February 19, 2003.

Bar-Yosef, Ofer, and David Pilbeam, eds. *The Geography of Neandertals and Modern Humans in Europe and the Greater Mediterranean.* Peabody Museum Bulletin 8. Cambridge, MA: Harvard University, 2000.

Bennett, Deborah J. *Logic Made Easy.* New York: Norton, 2004.

Bennett, J. M., and C. W. Hollister. *Medieval Europe: A Short History.* New York: McGraw-Hill, 2006.

Carlsson, M., G. B. Dahl, B. Öckert, and D.-O. Rooth, D.-O. The Effect of Schooling on Cognitive Skills. *Review of Economics and Statistics* 97, no. 3 (2015): 533–47.

Carr, Geoffrey. The Proper Study of Mankind. *The Economist*, December 24, 2005.

Chown, Marcus. Our World May Be a Giant Hologram. *New Scientist*, Issue 2691, January 15, 2009.

Clifford, William Kingdon. *Lectures and Essays by the Late William Kindon Clifford, F.R.S.* 2nd ed. Edited by Leslie Stephen and Frederick Pollock, with an introduction by F. Pollock. London: Macmillan, 1886.

Collaer, M. L., and M. Hines. Human Behavioural Sex Differences: A Role for Gonadal Hormones during Early Development? *Psychological Bulletin* 118, no. 1 (1995): 55–77.

Darwin, Charles. *The Illustrated Origin of Species.* Abridged, with an introduction by Richard Leakey. New York: Hill and Wang, 1982.

Davis, H. Prediction and Preparation: Pavlovian Implications of Research Animals Discriminating among Humans. *ILAR Journal* 43 (2002): 19–26.

Deacon, Terrence W. *The Symbolic Species: The Co-evolution of Language and the Brain.* New York: Norton, 1997.

Dennett, Daniel C. *Consciousness Explained.* Boston: Little, Brown, 1991.

de Waal, Franz. *Our Inner Ape.* New York: Penguin, 2005.

DiCarlo, Christopher. Critical Notice of Anthony O'Hear's *Beyond Evolution: Human Nature and the Limits of Evolutionary Explanation. Biology and Philosophy* 16, no. 1 (2000): 117–30.

———. The Influence of Selection Pressures and Secondary Epigenetic Rules on the Cognitive Development of Specific Forms of Reasoning. *Journal of Consciousness Studies: Consciousness Research Abstracts* (2000).

———. The Evolution of Morality. *Humanist in Canada*, no. 143 (Winter 2002/2003): 12–19.

———. *A Practical Guide to Thinking Critically.* Oshawa: McGraw-Hill Ryerson, 2007.

———. The Roots of Skepticism: Why Ancient Ideas Still Apply Today. *Skeptical Inquirer* 33, no. 3 (May/June 2009): 51–55.

———. The Co-Evolution of Consciousness and Language and the Development of Memetic Equilibrium. *Journal of Consciousness Exploration and Research* 1, no. 4 (June 2010): 410–28.

———. How Problem Solving and Neurotransmission in the Upper Paleolithic Led to the Emergence and Maintenance of Memetic Equilibrium in Contemporary World Religions. Special issue of *Politics and Culture*, Issue 1, April 27, 2010.

———. We Are All African: Can a Scientific Understanding of Our Commonality Save Us? *Free Inquiry*, June/July 2010, 18–22.

———. *How to Become a Really Good Pain in the Ass: A Critical Thinker's Guide to Asking the Right Questions.* Amherst, NY: Prometheus Books, 2011.

———. How to Avoid a Robotic Apocalypse: A Consideration on the Future Developments of AI, Emergent Consciousness, and the Frankenstein Effect. *IEEE Technology and Society Magazine* 35, no. 4 (2016): 56–61.

DiCarlo, Christopher, and John Teehan. On the Naturalistic Fallacy: A Conceptual Basis for Evolutionary Ethics. *Evolutionary Psychology: An International Journal of Evolutionary Approaches to Psychology and Behavior* 2 (March 2004): 32–46.

Doidge, Norman. *The Brain That Changes Itself.* New York: Penguin, 2007.

Dunbar, Robin. *Grooming, Gossip and Language.* Cambridge, MA: Harvard University Press, 1998.

Festinger, L., Henry Riecken, and Stanley Schachter. *When Prophecy Fails: A Social and Psychological Study of a Modern Group That Predicted the Destruction of the World.* New York: Harper Torchbooks, 1956.

Frederikse, M. E., A. Lu, E. Aylward, P. Barta, and G. Pearlson. Sex Differences in the Inferior Parietal Lobule. *Cerebral Cortex* 9, no. 8 (1999): 896–901.

Gavrilets, Sergey, and William R. Rice. Genetic Models of Homosexuality: Generating Testable Predictions. *Proceedings of the Royal Society* 273, no. 1605 (December 2006): 3031–38.

Goodman, Felix. *The Evolution and Function of Cognition.* Mahwah, NJ: Lawrence Erlbaum Associates, 2003.

Hale, John R., et al. Questioning the Delphic Oracle. *Scientific American*, August 2003.

Hallie, Philip P. *Sextus Empiricus: Selections from the Major Writings on Scepticism, Man, and God.* Indianapolis: Hackett, 1985.

Halpern, D. F. Teaching Critical Thinking for Transfer across Domains: Disposition, Skills, Structure Training, and Metacognitive Monitoring. *American Psychologist* 53, no. 4 (1998): 449–55.

Hamilton, W. D. The Evolution of Altruistic Behavior. *American Naturalist* 97 (1963): 354–56.

Hamm, Robert M. No Effect of Intercessory Prayer Has Been Proven." *Archives of Internal Medicine* 160, no. 12 (2000): 1872–73.

Hammerschmidt, Dale E. "Ethical and Practical Problems in Studying Prayer." *Archives of Internal Medicine* 160, no. 12 (2000): 1874–75.

Harari, Yuval Noah. *Sapiens: A Brief History of Humankind.* London: Harvill Secker, 2014.

———. *Homo Deus: A Brief History of Tomorrow.* London: Harvill Secker, 2016.

———. *21 Lessons for the 21st Century.* London: Jonathan Cape, 2018.

Hare, R. M. *Freedom and Reason.* Oxford: Oxford University Press, 1963.

Harris, Sam. *The Moral Landscape.* New York: Free Press, 2010.

Hawking, Stephen, and Leonard Mlodinow. *The Grand Design.* New York: Bantam Books, 2010.

Heijltjes, A., T. Van Gog, and F. Paas. Improving Students' Critical Thinking: Empirical Support for Explicit Instructions Combined with Practice. *Applied Cognitive Psychology* 28, no. 4 (2014): 518–30.

Helsdingen, A. S., K. van den Bosch, T. van Gog, and J. J. G. van merrienboer. The Effects of Critical Thinking Instruction on Training Complex Decision Making. *Human Factors* 52, no. 4 (2010): 537–45.

Hume, David. *Essays on Suicide and the Immortality of the Soul.* Unauthorized ed., 1783.

———. *An Inquiry concerning Human Understanding.* New York: Macmillan, 1989.

Kellert, Stephen R., and E. O. Wilson, eds. *The Biophilia Hypothesis.* Washington, DC: Island Press, 1993.

Kübler-Ross, Elizabeth. *Death and Dying.* New York: Simon & Schuster, 1969.

Kuhn, D., and A. Crowell. Dialogic Argumentation as a Vehicle for Developing Young Adolescents' Thinking. *Psychological Science* 22, no. 4 (2011): 545–52.

Kurtz, K. J., O. Boukrina, and D. Gentner. Comparison Promotes Learning and Transfer of Relational Categories. *Journal of Experimental Psychology: Learning, Memory, and Cognition* 39, no. 4 (2013): 1303–10.

Levitt, Steven, and Stephen J. Dubner. *Freakonomics: A Rogue Economist Explores the Hidden Side of Everything.* New York: William Morrow/Harper-Collins, 2005.

Lieberman, P. *The Biology and Evolution of Language.* Cambridge, MA: Harvard University Press, 1984.

Macaskill, William. *Doing Good Better.* New York: Penguin Random House, 2015.

McCleery, Iona. Medical Miracles: Doctors, Saints, and Healing in the Modern World. *New England Journal of Medicine* 360 (2009): 2261–62.

McDougall, Duncan. Hypothesis concerning Soul Substance Together with Experimental Evidence of the Existence of such Substance. *Journal of the American Society for Psychical Research* 1, no. 5 (May 1905): 237–75.

Mlodinow, Leonard. *The Drunkard's Walk: How Randomness Rules Our Lives.* New York: Random House, 2008.

Moir, Anne, and David Jessel. *Brain Sex: The Real Difference between Men and Women.* New York: Bantam Doubleday Dell Publishing, 1992.

Moody, Raymond. *Life after Life: The Investigation of a Phenomenon—Survival of Bodily Death.* San Francisco: Harper, 2001.

Nagel, Thomas. "What Is It Like to Be a Bat? *Philosophical Review* 83, no. 4 (1974): 435–50.

Pande, Prakash N. Does Prayer Need Testing? *Archives of Internal Medicine* 160, no. 12 (2000): 1873–74.

Pinker, S. *How the Mind Works.* New York: Norton, 2009.

———. *The Better Angels of Our Nature.* New York: Viking, 2011.

———. *The Blank Slate* (2002/2016). New York: Viking, 2016.

———. *Enlightenment Now: The Case for Reason, Science, Humanism, and Progress.* New York: Viking, 2018.

Plato. *The Apology.* From *Readings in Ancient Greek Philosophy: From Thales to Aristotle.* 2nd ed. Indianapolis: Hackett, 2000.

Price, John M. Does Prayer Really Set One Apart? *Archives of Internal Medicine* 160, no. 12 (2000): 1873.

Ridley, Matt. *Nature via Nurture: Genes, Experience, and What Makes Us Human.* Toronto: HarperCollins, 2003.

Ritchie, S. J., and E. M. Tucker-Drob. How Much Does Education Improve Intelligence? A Meta-Analysis. *Psychological Science* 29, no. 8 (2018): 1358–69.

Romero, G., et al. How Accurate Is the Current Picture of Human Genetic Variation? *Heredity* 102 (2009): 120–26.

Rosner, Fred. Therapeutic Efficacy of Prayer. *Archives of Internal Medicine* 160, no. 12 (2000): 1875.

Roy, David J., et al. *Bioethics in Canada*. Scarborough: Prentice Hall, 1994.

Sackett, D. L. Bias in Analytic Research. *Journal of Chronic Diseases* 32 (1979): 51–63.

Sapolsky, Robert. Taming Stress. *Scientific American* 289, no. 3 (September 2003): 87–95.

Sapolsky, Robert, and Rupshi Mitra. Effects of Enrichment Predominate over Those of Chronic Stress on Fear-Related Behavior in Male Rats. *Stress* 12, no. 4 (2009): 305–12.

Schwitzgebel, E., and F. Cushman. Philosophers' Biased Judgments Persist despite Training, Expertise and Reflection. *Cognition* 141 (2015): 127–37.

Shermer, Michael. *Why People Believe Weird Things*. New York: Henry Holt, 2002.

Sloan, Richard P., and Emilia Bagiella. Data without a Prayer. *Archives of Internal Medicine* 160, no. 12 (2000): 1870.

Sylvester, Robert. How Emotions Affect Learning. *Education Leadership* 52, no. 2 (October 1994): 60–65.

Taatgen, N. A. The Nature and Transfer of Cognitive Skills. *Psychological Review* 120, no. 3 (2013): 439–71.

Tattersall, Ian. Once We Were Not Alone. *Scientific American: New Look at Human Evolution*, June 2003, 20–27.

Van der Does, Willem. A Randomized, Controlled Trial of Prayer? *Archives of Internal Medicine* 160, no. 12 (2000): 1871–72.

Vincent, J. D. 1990. *The Biology of Emotions*. Cambridge, MA: Basil Blackwell.

Waterhouse, William C. Is It Prayer, or Is It Parity? *Archives of Internal Medicine* 160, no. 12 (2000): 1875.

Watson, J. D., and F. H. C. Crick, A Structure for Deoxyribose Nucleic Acid. *Nature* 171 (1953): 737–38.

Wattles, Jeff. *The Golden Rule*. New York: Oxford University Press, 1996.

Whiten, Andrew. Social Complexity and Social Intelligence. *Novartis Foundation Symposium* 233 (2000): 185–96.

Whiten, Andrew, and Christophe Boesch. The Cultures of Chimpanzees. *Scientific American*, January 2001, 60–67.

Willingham, D. T. Critical Thinking: Why Is It So Hard to Teach? *American Educator*, Summer 2007, 8–19.

———. *When Can You Trust the Experts? How to Tell Good Science from Bad in Education*. San Francisco: Jossey-Bass, 2012.

———. Education: Future Frontiers. How to Teach Critical Thinking. 2019. https://education.nsw.gov.au/media/exar/How-to-teach-critical-thinking -Willingham.pdf.

Wrangham, Richard W., James Holland Jones, Greg Laden, David Pilbeam, and NancyLou Conklin-Brittain. Cooking and the Ecology of Human Origins. *Current Anthropology* 40 (1999): 567–94.

Yeh, G. Y., et al. Use of Complementary and Alternative Medicine among Persons with Diabetes Mellitus: Results of a National Survey. *American Journal of Public Health* 92, no. 10 (2002): 1648–52.

Zimmer, Carl. *Evolution: The Triumph of an Idea.* New York: HarperCollins, 2001.

Index

About the Author

Christopher DiCarlo, PhD, is a philosopher, educator, and author. He often teaches at the University of Toronto and Ryerson University. He is a past visiting research scholar at Harvard University. He has been invited to speak at numerous national and international conferences and written many scholarly peer-reviewed papers ranging from bioethics to cognitive evolution. He has been awarded TV Ontario's *Big Ideas* Best Lecturer in Ontario Award. Currently, he is the ethics chair for the Canadian Mental Health Association (Waterloo/Wellington) as well as the principal and founder of Critical Thinking Solutions, a consulting business for individuals, corporations, and not-for-profits in both the private and the public sector. He also holds the position of critical thinking advisor and writer at Pixel Dreams Creative Agency in Toronto, Ontario. He is the author of *How to Become a Really Good Pain in the Ass: A Critical Thinker's Guide to Asking the Right Questions* (2011).